Cornelius A. Moloney

West African Fisheries

with particular reference to the Gold Coast Colony

Cornelius A. Moloney

West African Fisheries
with particular reference to the Gold Coast Colony

ISBN/EAN: 9783337123550

Printed in Europe, USA, Canada, Australia, Japan

Cover: Foto ©Andreas Hilbeck / pixelio.de

More available books at **www.hansebooks.com**

International Fisheries Exhibition

LONDON 1883

WEST AFRICAN FISHERIES

WITH PARTICULAR REFERENCE TO

THE GOLD COAST COLONY

BY

Captain C. A. MOLONEY, C.M.G.

" Bait the hook well; this fish will bite."

" It is lawful for you to fish in the sea, and to eat what ye shall catch, as a provision for you and for those who travel."

LONDON

WILLIAM CLOWES AND SONS, Limited

13 CHARING CROSS, S.W.

1883

International Fisheries Exhibition,

LONDON, 1883.

CONFERENCE ON 24TH OCTOBER, 1883.

ON WEST AFRICAN FISHERIES, WITH PARTICULAR REFERENCE TO THE GOLD COAST COLONY.

IN explanation of my acceptance of the invitation of the Executive Committee of the International Fisheries Exhibition to write a Paper on " West African Fisheries, with particular reference to the Gold Coast Colony," I must ask to be allowed to preface what follows by an acknowledgment of the fact that whatever knowledge of the subject I may possess is confined mostly to the breakfast and dinner table ; and I am doubtful whether in my shallowness or taste I am an exception.

When I ventured to undertake this Paper, it naturally first occurred to look about for information, and to thus endeavour to reap a harvest on the brains of others ; but to my inquiry of unscientific and worldly friends as to what they knew of the fish fauna, the invariable answer I received was—"At present, my dear fellow, cod is in season," or some like communication. "As regards that awful place West Africa, comparatively nothing has been written, for the general belief is that even fish won't live there."

Now, on the contrary, much has been written. The fauna literature applicable to West Africa is extensive, although scattered, and I am, in consequence of limited

B 2

time, and of appreciation for the patience of my kind listeners, unable to carry out an original intention to refer in detail to it; yet I may hurriedly allude, as convenient references for any future enthusiastic disciples, to—

The 'Geographical Distribution of the Zoological Record.'

Günther's 'Catalogue of Fishes.'

Günther's 'Study of Fishes.'

Dr. Savage's 'Study of the Ichthyological Fauna of the Ogooué' (in Gaboon), 1880.

Dr. Rochebrune's 'Fish Fauna of the Senegambia,' 1883.

To our shame, zoological work and its record are making headway in other Possessions than our own. Look to the admirable works just quoted of Doctors Savage and Rochebrune. They have but recently come into my hands, so that time, even if space did so, will not admit of my taking advantage of them.

Of the zoological division of the earth's surface as proposed by Mr. Sclater, the Ethiopian region stands forth as including Africa south of Sahara, Madagascar, and the Mascerene Islands, also southern Arabia.

Then again as to the fauna of fresh-water fishes, Dr. Günther has proposed the division into zones, among which stands the equatorial zone, noted by the development of Siluridæ, and characterised as far as the African region is concerned by the presence also of *Dipnoi* and *Polypteridæ*, *Chromides* and *Characinidæ*, being numerous, with *Mormyridæ* present and *Cobitidæ* absent.

This authority has further divided the equatorial zone into four regions, one being described as African, with which we have now more to do than with any other, but which cannot according to him well be treated as to its fish fauna as absolutely distinct; for there "exists, for instance, a great affinity between the Indian and African regions ; seventeen out of the twenty-six families or groups found in the former are represented by one or more species in Africa, and many of the African species are not even generically different from the Indian," and as the majority of these groups have many more representatives in India than in Africa, it has been assumed "that the African species have been derived from the Indian" stock, but even to such an assumption there are exceptions.

The African fresh-water region comprises, according to Dr. Günther's arrangement, the whole of the African continent south of the Atlas and the Sahara, but for the purpose of this Paper, in which I treat of the marine fauna as well, I would dwell generally on the western coast line of that Continent lying between 30° N. lat. and 35° S. lat., for within such latitudes lie not only the coast line and adjacent waters, but also the Canaries, Cape Verde Islands, Fernando Po, Princes Island, St. Thomas and Annobon, to which I would like to make a brief reference.

I am, apart from interest, the more induced to so act as "the difference between the tropical and southern parts of Africa consists simply in the gradual disappearance of specifically tropical forms, whilst *Siluroids, Cyprinoids,* and even *Labyrinthici,*" which are peculiar to the warmer latitudes "penetrate to its southern coast"; thus "no new form entering to impart to South Africa a character distinct from the central portion of its Continent."

Whilst deciding not to encompass in this Paper widely spread comparisons even as far as the African region goes, extending in the north-east as to its fauna by the Isthmus of Suez into Syria, "the system of the Jordan presenting so many African types that it has to be included in a description of the African region, as well as of the Europo-Asiatic," I may say that two hundred and fifty-five species of known fresh-water forms inhabit it, contracted into thirty-nine families or groups, of which fifteen are represented in the African, as against twelve in the Indian region. Further, the African species, as compared with the Indian, are represented in the proportion of two to five, due, it is advanced, to the greater uniformity of the physical condition of the African continent, and to the almost perfect continuity of the great river systems, which take their origin from the lakes in the centre.

"This," says Dr. Günther, "is best shown by a comparison of the fauna of the Upper Nile with that of the West African rivers. The number of species known from the Upper Nile amounts to fifty-six, and of these not less than twenty-five are absolutely identical with West African species. There is an uninterrupted continuity of the fish fauna from west to the north-east, and the species known to be common to both extremities may be reasonably assumed to inhabit also the great reservoirs of water in the centre of the continent. A greater dissimilarity is noticeable between the west and north-east fauna on the one hand and that of the Zambezi on the other; the affinity between them is merely generic; and all the fishes hitherto collected in Lake Nyassa have proved to be distinct from those of the Nile, and even from those of other parts of the system of the Zambezi."

"Africa, unlike India, does not possess either alpine ranges or outlying archipelagoes, the fresh waters of which would swell the number of its indigenous species; but at a future time, when its fauna is better known than at present, it is possible that the great difference in the number of species between this and the Indian regions may be somewhat lessened."

To give a more extended but brief comparison of the fresh-water fauna of the African, as against the other regions, I would quote that:

"The regions with which Africa (like India) has least similarity are, again, the North American and Antarctic. Its affinity with the Europo-Asiatic region consists only in having received, like this latter, a branch of the *Cyprinoids,* the African Carps and Barbels resembling, on the whole, more Indian than Europo-Asiatic forms. Its similarity to Australia is limited to the two regions possessing *Dipnoous* and *Osteoglossoid* types. But its relations to the two other regions of the equatorial zone are near and of great interest."

And in the affinity of the fresh-water fishes, as regards Africa and South America, I must trespass on your patience by asking to be allowed to read as follows :

" The existence of so many similar forms on both sides of the Atlantic affords much support to the supposition that at a former period the distance between the present Atlantic continents was much less, and that the fishes which have diverged towards the East and West are descendants of a common stock, which had its home in a region now submerged under some intervening part of that ocean. Be this as it may, it is evident that the physical conditions of Africa and South America have remained unchanged for a considerable period, and are still sufficiently alike to preserve the identity of a number of peculiar fresh-water forms on both sides of the Atlantic. Africa and South America are, moreover, the only continents which have produced in fresh-water fishes, though in very different families, one of the most extraordinary modifications of an organ—the conversion, that is, of muscle into an apparatus creating electric force."

The lagoons, or inland waterways, that run parallel to the sea, especially on the Guinea coast, presenting, as regards their formation, such an interesting geological study, afford a grand and rich field for the study of the brackish-water fauna, among which are mentioned, so far as I may specially give, in connection with the equatorial zone, the *Raiidæ, Sciænidæ, Polynemidæ, Caranx, Chatoessus, Megalops,* and *Syngathidæ.*

Of lagoons I may give here the opinion of the authors of ' To the Gold Coast for Gold,' which is expressed as follows :

"The formation of these characteristic African features, which either run parallel with, or are disposed at various angles to the coast, is remarkably simple. There is no reason to assume with Lieutenant R. C. Hart that they result from secular upheaval (page 186, Gold Coast Blue Book, London, 1881). The 'powerful artillery with which the ocean assails the bulwarks of the land, here heaps up a narrow strip of high sand bank, and the toils of the smaller streams are powerless to break through it, except when swollen by the rains. They maintain their level by receiving fresh water at the head, and by percolation through the beach, while most of them are connected with the sea."

Next as to marine fishes. Of the shore-fish—term applied to the fish inhabitants of the immediate neighbourhood of land either actually raised above, or at least but little submerged below the surface of the water—of the equatorial zone, Dr. Günther states that as regards the tropical Atlantic and Indo-Pacific fauna, the differences are far less numerous and important than between the fresh-water or terrestrial fauna of continental regions. The majority of the principal types are found in both, many of the species being even identical; but the species are far more abundant in the Indo-Pacific than in the Atlantic, which is attributed to the greater extent of archipelagoes in the former. He continues—

"But for the broken and varied character of the coasts of the West Indies, the shores of the tropical Atlantic would, by their general uniformity, afford but a limited variety of conditions to the development of specific and generic forms, whilst the deep inlets of the Indian Ocean, with the varying configuration of their coasts, and the different nature of their bottoms, its long peninsulas and its archipelagoes, and the scattered islands of the tropical Pacific, render these parts of the globe the most perfect for the development of fish life."

"The boundaries of the tropical Atlantic extend zoologically a few degrees beyond the northern and southern tropics; but as the mixture with the types of the temperate zone is very gradual, no distinct boundary line can be drawn between the tropical and temperate faunæ.

" Types almost exclusively limited to the tropical Atlantic, and not found in the Indo-Pacific, are few in number, as *Centropristis*, *Rhypticus*, *Hæmulon*, *Malthe*. A few others preponderate with regard to the number of species, as *Plectropoma*, *Sargus*, *Trachynotus*, *Batrachidæ*, and *Gobiesocidæ*. The *Sciænoids* are equally represented in both oceans. All the remainder are found in both, but in the minority in the Atlantic, where they are sometimes represented by one or two species only (for instance, *Lethrinus*)."

It would seem that—

" As with fresh-water fishes, the main divisions of the shore-fish fauna are determined by their distance from the equator, the equatorial zone of the fresh-water series corresponding entirely to that of the shore-fish series."

Although as regards the latter, the fauna is more extended north and south in its distribution from the equator.

Dr. Günther's ' Study of Fishes ' affords, from page 275, a list which, although only containing the principal genera or groups of coast-fishes, in the Equatorial zone, yet admits of the formation of an opinion on the affinity of the Tropical Atlantic and Indo-Pacific, and to it, for more detailed information generally in what I have ventured to extract, I would beg leave to refer my hearers.

There are included in the list ninety-six families or groups of shore-fishes in connection with the Tropical Atlantic and the Indo-Pacific, in the proportion of 59 to 87, and although these are not specimens of each genus common, yet the proportion of the species stands as 532 to 1917.

Pelagic fishes, viz., fishes inhabiting the surface of mid-ocean, like shore-fishes, are most numerous in the tropical zone, and with few exceptions—*Echinorhinus*, *Psenes*,

Sternoptychidæ, Astronesthes—the same genera occupy the Tropical Atlantic as well as the Indo-Pacific.

"The pelagic fauna of the tropics gradually passes into that of the temperate zones, only a few genera, like *Cybium, Psenes* and *Antennarius*, being almost entirely confined to the tropics."

Among the fish off and within this coast line, I may explain ordinarily, are met sharks, cat-fish, albacore, bonito, rays, blennies, barracouta, grey mullet, ctenopoma allied to the climbing perch, the "fighting fish," flat-fish, carp, flying fish, electric fish, herring, anchovy, mud-fish, eels, "shine-noze," "rock cod," sun fish, "globe fish," perch, mackerel, sword-fish, dolphin, pilchard, &c.

Most of the works one takes up on this part of Africa point to the importance of the fresh-water fish industry as a means of support for the natives, and many allude to the grand sea-fish field represented by the tropical Eastern Atlantic.

Bosman, in his 'Coast of Guinea,' written nearly two hundred years ago, affords particulars of the value of sea and fresh-water fish to the natives.

Tucker, in his 'Narrative on Expedition to the River Zaire,' dwells upon the "swarms" of albacore, bonito, and other fish met with in the Gulf of Guinea, on the voyage in 1816 of the "Congo," as also of the importance and richness of the fish field of the river of same name (the then Zaire, now Congo).

Bowdich and Dupuis testify to the quantity of fish to be met with in the rivers of the Ashantee kingdom and of the other surrounding countries, and of its necessity as an article of food.

Bowen, in his interesting 'Central Africa,' alludes to frequently seeing fish exposed for sale in different interior markets of the Yoruba kingdom, and to the richness of its streams in this commodity.

The importance of the fisheries in that part of the world and their growth did not escape the notice of the Select Committee of the House of Commons on the West Coast of Africa (1842), when Mr. Swanzy, of the firm bearing his name, conveyed that there was a great deal of fishing there, and that it "forms, as well as salt, a great article of commerce between the waterside and interior people."

Of the country behind the Portuguese Possessions in South-West Africa, Messrs. Capello and Ivens in their "from Benguela to Yacca," state of the river Luando, "it is extremely abundant in fish; its banks are visited by numerous tribes, who devote their attention to fishing, using for this purpose the 'mu-ghande,' snares of various kinds." "So abundantly is this river supplied that, as we were assured, it furnishes, jointly with the lakes of Qui-honde and Catete, more to the north, and the Njombo, one of its affluents, sufficient fish for the large requirements of the Songo country."

Schweinfurth, in his 'Heart of Africa,' alludes frequently to the plentifulness of fish in the rivers in tropical Africa which lay in his path, and also records the abundance of crocodiles and hippopotami. Writing of the modes of capture adopted by the natives, he states:—" They proceed very much in the European way of damming up the stream by weirs, and laying down wicker pots of considerable size. The fishing, for the most part, is done twice a year, first at the commencement of the rainy season, and again when the waters begin to subside."

The importance that attaches to certain of the Ganoids (of which so many specimens are extinct, and are of great geological interest), such as *Protopterus annectens, Polyp-*

terus Senegalus, Calamoichthys, induces me to briefly mention them here. The first abounds in many places, and forms an important article of food. It is to be frequently seen at the native markets in a smoked condition, almost black, and secured in numbers in circular form on bamboo skewers.

As to deep-sea fishes, viz., those which inhabit such depths of the ocean as to be but little or not influenced by light or the surface temperature, I do not feel, in view of object and scope of this Paper, called upon to dwell.

Philanthropic and scientific expeditions undertaken at various times in the past, point to the fertility of the Eastern Atlantic as a fish-bed, but it is evident that sufficient advantage, compared with the fruit to have been reaped, has not been taken of nature's bounty; and as regards West Africa, a comparatively new and scientifically unknown region, other mercantile and more popular attractions and manias have caused the fish industry to be now what it was a hundred years ago, aye, more, *ab initio*, the primitive calling and promotion of the aborigines in whose hands it has been and is, but towards whom more interest of a practical nature should have been, and, it is to be hoped, will be directed in the matter, at least, of the improvement of the system of catch and healthy supply.

West African Settlements.

The West African Settlements, commonly understood as Sierra Leone and the Gambia, were reconstituted under Letters Patent of the 17th December, 1874, into one Government, comprising Her Majesty's Settlement of Sierra Leone, embracing all places, settlements, and territories which may at any time belong to Her Majesty in West Africa between the 6th and 12th degrees of N. latitude and lying to the westward of the 10th degree of W. longitude, and Her Majesty's Settlement on the Gambia, comprising all places, settlements, and territories which may at any time belong to Her Majesty in West Africa, between the 12th and 15th degrees of N. latitude, and lying to the westward of the 10th degree of W. longitude.

The population of the British Settlements on the Gambia was given, in 1881, as 14,150, of whom 105 were Europeans, including crews of ships in harbour. Of the total, 296 were returned as fishermen and native seamen, whose pursuits are mainly, if not altogether, confined to the river Gambia.

On the Gambia fisheries, the Blue Books say that "there are none except for the daily table supply, which is varied and abundant. Canoes are employed in fishing."

The values of imports for 1880 and 1881 are returned as £191,580 and £142,589. These figures include £735 and £1,205 as value of imported salt. Information is not particularised of the introduction of any foreign fish.

The population of Sierra Leone and its dependencies was given, in 1881, as 60,546, of whom 271 were whites, inclusive of 108 crews of vessels in harbour. Of this total there were 1,964 fishermen and native seamen, on whom the Colonial Secretary reported as follows :—

"Of the fishermen and native seamen, who number nearly 2,000, more than half may be said to be fishermen, who, beyond providing themselves and their families with the means of subsistence, contribute but little to the comforts of the inhabitants, and practically nothing to the State. The native seamen, taken all round, are an ill-paid and ill-conditioned class, who endure many hardships, and who appear to have at present but a slight chance of ameliorating their condition."

The value of imports for 1880 and 1881 are returned as £491,993 and £374,375. These figures include £781 and £336 value of imported fish, as also £4,145 and £2,930 for introduced salt. Boats and canoes, licensed in 1880 and 1881, were 689 and 572.

It would be unnecessary and unimportant to give here the local names of fish. You will be amused, but not enlightened, to hear that some are "Blue Billies," others "Black Billies," information which would defy, for the purpose of classification, the ingenuity of any fish Authority.

French West African Settlements.

As to the French Possessions, generally referred to as Senegambia, Gaboon, and Assinee, with a returned population (1878) of 324,038, I know of no systematic fish industry beyond, perhaps, the requirements for a hand-to-mouth existence and precarious inland trade.

Gold Coast Colony.

It is very difficult to form an estimate as to the numbers of any native population of a somewhat migratory character and of a Protectorate, for we must remember that Her Majesty's Settlements on the Gold Coast are represented by " Colony " and " Protected Territories," the statements alone of natives as to numbers being uncertain, and, I may say, quite unreliable.

Then, again, natives are peculiarly suspicious, and would be disposed to be at once on their guard against supplying information which they would view as intended to be directed against themselves in the shape of taxation, perhaps conscription, as was fancied at places in the Ashantee War, 1873-4.

No approximate value of the fisheries can be given.

Data are not forthcoming. The population of the Gold
Coast cannot, it would seem, be got within the range of
"practical statistics." It will be ideal to state that most of
the people, estimated in round numbers say at 400,000, live
chiefly on fish, so that some conception can be formed of
the considerable catch there must be annually to supply
such a mass, as also the great unlimited interior markets
beyond our jurisdiction.

The Gold Coast Colony—prior to the following date
made up of the Settlements on the Gold Coast and the
Settlement of Lagos—comprises, according to Letters Patent
of 22nd January, 1883, all places, settlements, and territories belonging to Her Majesty the Queen in West Africa,
between the 5th degree of W. longitude and the 5th degree
of E. longitude. It must not be understood that the colony
is one and undivided, for a strip of coast and country commonly known as the Dahomean sea-board and territory
intervenes.

The population of the Gold Coast has, as already stated,
never yet got beyond an estimate. Lagos was, however,
more favoured, for in 1881 the census effort there applied
and gave its population as 75,270, inclusive of 117 whites
and 68 mulattos, of whom 5,695 were returned as fishermen.

In view of what I have explained, it will be very evident
that it would simply be farcical to endeavour to foist on to
you any estimate of catch or of cure ; indeed, such particulars are not arrived at even in England. But against
whatever may be the consumption of locally-caught and
preserved fish, it may be interesting to have, by way of
comparison, the value of what has been imported of this
article—which I give for four years :—

Year.	Value of fish imported. Gold Coast.	Value of fish imported. Lagos.	Value of total imports. Gold Coast.	Value of total imports. Lagos.
	£. s. d.	£. s. d.	£.	£.
1878	370 0 5	176 3 2	394,152	483,623
1879	174 15 10	435 9 1	323,039	527,871
1880	No statistics.	576 9 0	337,248	376,215
1881	248 1 11	273 15 8	398,123	336,659

There has been no exportation of fish—naturally. Imported fish, which is brought mainly from the United Kingdom, Germany, and America, is chiefly represented by tinned and smoked salmon, lobster, sardines, salt cod and ling, red herrings, and mackerel, and is supplied to meet the taste of Europeans and Europeanized natives. The aborigines, as a rule, prefer their own fish, as will be explained later.

For my own part, I would not be prepared to view these statistics as giving the fishing population, for natives often combine the work of farming with fishing. There are, of course, some who are merely fishermen and nothing more, or rather, when they are anything more, they are idlers; although I am glad to acknowledge I have seen many an exception to this, in men who have turned, and do turn during leisure time, their hands to some other remunerative work than fishing; while there are others—and a large number—who do not confine themselves to fishing as a sole means of livelihood, but as a subsidiary occupation. Idleness, notwithstanding, prevails much, but this may be excusable in view of absence of competition as regards production, as also of conditions of climate, and the, fortunately for them, small demand made on them towards food provision, Nature having been, and being, so bountiful.

The fishing craft is represented altogether by the canoe, "the dug-out," of varying sizes, regulated by the number of persons carried, viz., from five to one. They are generally hollowed out, by the adze and burning of the trunk, of the silk cotton (*Bombax*), or of a species of fig. Canoes most frequently used are those for three persons; they are propelled by paddles, the shapes of which vary tribally, the occupant (or occupants) resting on his knees, on his haunches, or standing erect, or perched on seats— cross sticks, secured by tie-tie on gunwale of canoe.

They are sometimes built up at the sides when required for commercial transport purposes, for ferry-boats or as war-canoes. The ordinary sized fishing canoe is propelled by three men, one of whom, occupying the stern, propels and steers, his main duty being the latter; and in their management of the craft they are surprisingly clever.

Transport is mainly effected by means of rivers and lagoons, viz., inland waterways, so far as water can be made use of, and on the heads of natives by land, as was experienced in the Ashantee war, 1873–4.

For water transport, canoes abound. The carrying power of canoes is judged by the number of persons or casks of oil each will carry. Their sizes accordingly vary from what can contain from two to eighty persons, or from two to sixteen puncheons of oil.

Bar-boats of seven to eight tons have been used at Lagos; only for commercial purposes, as the means for the transfer of cargoes from ship to shore, and of produce from shore to ship. They have been only used by the mercantile houses, but since the African Steamship Companies have supplied to Lagos and the rivers their own branch steamers, the number of bar-boats have considerably decreased, and their use is daily becoming a thing of the past.

Sea fishermen usually pursue their avocations in the day; they rarely work at night; but to this rule there are exceptions, while in the lagoons fresh-water fishing is conducted at times both day and night.

On moonlight nights, when fishing is conducted on the inland waters or rivers, the men make use of a piece of glass—broken bottle—and metal, thereby making a musical tinkle to attract the fish before the hand net is cast.

Sea fishermen, as I have said, rarely work at night. They usually start to fish at daybreak, and return about two or three o'clock in the afternoon. They are received on the beach by a large crowd, comprised of purchasers in the person of subsequent retailers and cooks : wives to witness the luck, children to carry back, as they had brought, the nets and fishing-gear and their fathers' spoil, scoffers to chaff in case of capsizing, or of return empty-handed. Canoes frequently capsize, having been caught broadside on by a roller, or at times they are turned completely round and then go over; the fishermen invariably hold on, right the canoe, bale her out, re-embark, and pursue what remains of their journey. When bad weather is expected, and they anticipate being capsized, the fishing-gear, as also their catch in reed bags, is secured to the cross-thwarts of the boat.

Sea fishermen act as a barometer, for their movements and energy depend somewhat on the weather and condition of the sea. I have often watched them repair to the beach, run out their canoes to the edge of the surf, make a few abortive efforts towards departure, shrug their shoulders, with a "not good enough" meaning, at the weather, their mind being at ease as to the morrow, by probably having had a good haul a day or two previous, run back their canoes, and return "not ingloriously" to their homes.

The fishermen, in costume for work, are almost in a state

of nature—and very wisely so—in view of the treacherous nature of surf, and of greater facility for paddling, and of less likelihood to contract disease. They are seen with a loin-cloth, of meagre dimensions, as a body cover, and for the head perhaps a broad-brimmed hat, or may be they are bareheaded. They take frequently with them their country clothes, a loose sheet-like body-covering wrapper, which, when worn, is carried toga-like, as illustrated in the views before us. These clothes may be seen on the return of the canoes wound around the head of their stalwart owners, to act as a sun-awning or umbrella. At times they are converted, as make-shifts, into temporary sails, although canoes are usually supplied with sheets of a like nature, or with sails made of fibre or leaf matting. The sail is square, or nearly so. There is a single mast—a bamboo pole—to the head of which the sail is either hoisted by means of a small line run through a hole made through the mast-head, or made fast with a seizing. The sail is spread by a bamboo "sprit," and is worked by means of a sheet and a brace on the sprit; usually one man holds these, while the other steers with a paddle, but sometimes one man performs both duties. There are occasions when the luff of the sail is "bowlined out" by means of another bamboo.

Very rarely accidents by drowning occur. · Of fishermen it might almost be said that they were amphibious. As children they are generally made pursue the calling of their fathers : they are to be seen all day long, especially in the heat of the day, in the water, either swimming, "turning turtle," engaged paddling a plank or remnant of a canoe, or learning the art of casting the net. In later years they frequently accompany their fathers, and learn their handicraft, and, when old enough, take to the industry themselves.

That West Africa affords a good stock for the development of a useful fish population may be inferred from the doings of their fellow-countrymen in the United States, where some 5,000 Negroes conduct chiefly the shad-fisheries, and "are employed during the shad and herring season in setting and hauling the seines." In the shore fisheries of Key West, Florida, Negroes "are considered among the most skilful of the sponge and market fishermen." Some Negroes are also to be found among the crews of the whaling vessels of Provincetown and New Bedford, United States, the latter alone representing over 200.

I must not forget the Kroo-boys — fine good-natured fellows, instinctively watermen, almost amphibious. Their native home is in the country of Sinou in the central part of the Republic of Liberia.* They are to be found all along the coast; in fact, I don't know what the coast would do without them. They are invaluable, and represent the most generally useful—whether ashore or afloat—and important tribe on the West Coast of Africa. Without them it would be difficult to work, on this malarial coast, our men-of-war, mail steamers, foreign vessels, all loading and unloading being done by them. I applied to them the term amphibious; well they are known, in fact it is a frequent practice, to swim off, pushing their casks of oil before them, from their own coast to trading vessels lying at anchor some one or two miles off. They are equally useful on shore.

Fisheries as to their economic value depend on quality, supply, and demand. Where a want equals the catch of

* Liberia with a coast line of some 600 miles, and extending inland some 100 miles, with a native population estimated at 1,068,000.

the finny tribe, an industry may be viewed as healthy, whether the supply be marketable and local, or whether—which is another consideration, and one more to the point as regards this Paper—local consumption or industrial demand, or both, does not equal the catch, and as a consequence the surplus has to be and can be profitably sent to more distant markets where disposal will readily follow. In the latter case so much would naturally depend on the available means and effective conveniences of transport, especially as to the disposition of fresh fish, or the effectiveness of curing where climate and circumstances put beyond consideration the transit of fresh fish. As a rule, it may be said of the tropics, that fresh fish, to be enjoyed, must be consumed on the day of the catch. It does not always admit, indeed, of this—and the surplus captures, if energy prove sufficient for such an issue, are cured and sent to inland markets that offer.

My remarks are meant to apply to the Gold Coast Colony, where the people may be described as a fish-eating population, and where caste prejudices do not exist. Fetish restrictions may be at times, but rarely, imposed on the catch or consumption of this article of diet, but charity begins at home even with the Fetishman—who is often a fisherman, and, when not, is the recipient of " dashes " from the sea in the shape of fish by the propitiators of the sea-god ; thus he would not be so short-sighted as to impose any restrictions on so needful and essential a commodity, especially when he would know that, were he to do so, his power of imposing obedience might be jeopardised by seafarers.

It may be as well to add here that sovereign water rights are at times exercised in Native States through the medium of a fetish—to wit—the "Adanve" over the Denham

waters,* which have been and are through its instrument-
ality, subject to the Government of the King of Katanu—
a right that has been recognised and acknowledged by
all the surrounding tribes.

Ponds of fish, the subject of worship, are to be at places
met with. Rivers also represent resorts, in the native mind,
of favourite fetishes. The fetish of the river Tando is a
favourite one of the Ashantees ; Cobee, a river in Denkera,
and Odentee in the Adirree, are two others.

The river " Dah," in Ashantee, receives annual ablutions
and offerings in thanks to its Fetish for the yam of the
year—the Adai custom.

The sea-god has also offerings and propitiatory attentions.

Of sea-fishing, I am unaware of any close season ; but
there are times when the fishing of some of the rivers and
lagoons is by fetish order forbidden, in reality to allow of
the growth of fish which is of general interest. Opening
ceremonies after such "close times" are interesting and
important events.

In a country where local demand keeps pace with the
population, and where the cost of fishing-gear is comparatively trivial, when it is remembered that the value of time
is not yet known, so that the estimate of labour in the
computation of outlay on appliances is not of much
moment, the question of supply may be said to be favour-
ably met ; whereas as to the demand, the sale-market is
large and wide enough, representing, as it does, a huge
interior, but a clammy and damp, at the same time hot
climate, bad roads, no other means of transport but in
baskets on the heads of natives, imperfect system of curing,
stand forth as obstacles, and indeed great ones, towards
the development and growth of a healthy inland fish traffic.

* Behind the Dahomean seaboard.

Natives object to travel by land at night, and there is no interior demand of such a nature as to make such an effort worthy of the trouble in a pecuniary sense. No grand central Billingsgates exist to which fish could be taken fresh, and be at once disposed of. There are, however, regular native appointed markets held on certain days of the month or week, where, with other articles, dried fish is taken for sale, whence it is for the most part procurable.

Operations for the capture of the different forms of marine and fresh-water life are conducted from the sea beach and banks of inland waters, but as a rule by canoes, and effected by the following means which, with perhaps certain modifications, to meet tribal tastes or progress, apply, I am led to believe, generally to the Gulf of Guinea ; in fact, a look at the specimens of fish gear from other tropical parts might justify a more extended application.

I may remark that the descriptions which follow refer more directly to the fishing gear of Lagos, of the Gold Coast Colony, miniature models and specimens of which I had collected, and have presented for show in the Royal International Fisheries Exhibition 1883 :—

Fish-traps—called in Popo language "Aja," and in Fantee "Inchabah"—open baskets of split bamboo, secured by tie-tie, of circular form, with two entrances, one at either end, when double, or with one when single. Size varies, but usually made 6 feet long and $2\frac{1}{2}$ feet deep.

These traps are generally placed at the end or approach of a fish passage, whether natural or artificial, over a likely feeding ground. Baskets are, of course, baited with fish, or some farinaceous and oily compound.

Drag-nets—called in Popo language "Aveh," to drag, and in Fantee "Chouee," to draw—made of pineapple or other fibre. Size varies, but usually made 10 feet long, with a breadth of 2½ feet.

These nets are used in shallow fresh water, 3 or 4 feet deep, where they are drawn by men.

Hand-nets, called in the Popo language "Gangdoh," and in Fantee "Ebowaugh." Size as to net and meshes varies. Made of pineapple or other native fibre, also of imported twine; of circular form, usually about 12 feet diameter at mouth. Length of net, 12 or 15 feet; to end of net is affixed what may be called the casting-rope of some five or six fathoms.

This net is universally known in tropical seas and used from canoes, in fresh water, from banks and from the beach. It is thrown by fishermen, by a circular motion of the body from left to right, on the water, where it sinks by means of a weighted outer edge. On drawing up the net, which is allowed to sink as far as the casting-rope will admit, the weighted edge closes, and thus secures any fish over which it may have fallen.

Shrimp basket, made of open bamboo work, secured by tie-tie; of circular shape, tapering from a base varying in diameter from 2 to 4 feet, to a point when a length is reached of 8 or 10 feet, or even more.

These baskets are secured to stake-poles or sticks, laid out in parallel lines of considerable length, of a diameter of 2 or three inches, and of length dependent on depth of water where used. I have met them in water from 3 to 12 feet, even more. The stakes are conveyed by canoes to the site for which they are intended, and there erected by being gradually worked into the bottom by mere manual labour, and it is surprising how firmly they hold. To each stake is secured, with a connecting string of tie-tie of some length, a shrimp basket, which acts as a " hat " to the stake when the tide is going out, as it is so placed to avoid rotting or entanglement. On the flow the basket is lowered into the current. Shrimps, in immense shoals, are carried by the tide into its open mouth, thence to the narrow end, where they are collected in large numbers. From this trap there is no escape. Before the turn, two or three times during the flow, the stakes are visited by the employés or owner, and the baskets cleared.

It is a curious sight to observe of an evening these lines of stakes topped by sea-gulls, all heading to the wind or breeze, when there is one—balmy breezes do not always blow in these regions—which make them their roost for the night.

The catching of shrimps at Lagos represents a very large and extensive industry. The season lies between December and April. The industry includes local consumption and interior trade.

For storage and inland traffic shrimps are smoked, or rather semi-cooked, as follows. A fireplace of mud is built either in or out of doors, and is represented by an open oval-shaped horseshoe mud bank or small wall, the interruption in the shape to continuity acting as the means for draught and for the insertion of fuel, the enclosed area being the receptacle for the fire. Its size is dependent on proportion of industry. Across the open top are laid green supporting sticks, on which rest the fish to be cured, the fire having been first started. The process, which equally applies to fish, so primitive, is really a combined system of roasting and smoking. When sufficiently cured, according to native ideas, they are stowed away in baskets, and kept by the fireside, to frustrate as much as possible effects of damp, until finally removed for transport up country to the inland markets. The curing process and the later retail represent industries in the hands almost altogether of women.

At present the ex-king and chiefs of Lagos hold the shrimp-fishing as a monopoly enjoyed before and since the cession in 1861 of their country to Her Majesty. The industry, as far as the catch goes, is worked by their respective retainers, who also benefit by a return from their employers of the privilege to reap the fruits of the catch of a proportionate number of stakes.

Hand-nets, called in Popo language "Anyah," made of fibre; average length of pole, 4 to 5 feet; diameter of net, 1 or 2 feet, and its depth 2 feet; size varies in circumference.

This net corresponds with our English landing-nets, being used for securing fish caught by hook and line.

Hand trawl-net, called in Popo language "Azohara," viz., horn-shaped net; length of supporting pole varies to 20 feet; base of triangle formed by horns about 6 feet wide; depth of net, 8 feet. Size varies. Some tough wood selected; net made of pine-apple or other native fibre, secured by tie-tie.

This net is used as a rule in fresh water from a canoe which is allowed to float with the stream, or may be paddled against it, the pole being immersed to its depth, and the netted end brought up under the banks, especially where grass abounds.

Nets for shrimp or fresh-water shell-fish, called in Popo language "Adada," to lift. Length of handle of net, 6 feet; dimensions of net, 2 feet by 4 feet, and 2 feet deep; size varies.

These nets are for a purpose similar to our landing-nets

in England. They are also used either in securing shrimps out of the shrimp-baskets, or under grassy banks of land-sheltered waters for shell-fish.

Matting or grating, called in Popo language " Gba," made of split bamboo, secured by tie-tie.

This matting is very generally used in shallow water, to encircle fishing or good feeding ground covered at high tide, or for encircling floating "grass islands" (really portions of grassy bank eaten and carried away by current or floods), which are first anchored, and which fish make a favourable resort as a feeding-ground; or in making passages into which to allure fish by means of the additional attraction of baited fish-traps at their ends.

The floating islands are not regarded as "flotsam and jetsam." Each can be secured by any person, whose property it then becomes; he stakes it and allows it to remain as a feeding-ground for some weeks, after which he encircles it with bamboo grating as described; the "island" is then cut to pieces and thrown out over the grating which is next gradually contracted so as to bring the fish enclosed, if any, within small compass, when such as may have been entrapped are removed by one of the hand-nets already described. This practice is also applied to grassy banks.

Passages 3 or 4 feet wide are also cut of considerable length into low-lying ground or marshy places; such are filled at the flood, when the entrances are blocked by bamboo grating. On the ebb the passage is free from water, and the fish collected.

Manatee-trap, called in Popo language "Whanh," generally erected in sheltered water 4 to 6 feet deep, and near or on the slope of a river or lagoon bank. Briefly described it is a harpoon of heavy wood tipped with iron, suspended by a string connected with a peg slightly secured in the feeding-passage, which is immediately under the weapon, from the cross-piece of a supporting wooden framework composed of hard wood and tie-tie.

This trap is generally placed amid rank grass through which a passage has been cleared. About the peg is deposited a small delicate grass known to the natives. During grazing, which is effected on its back, the animal displaces the catch, and meets his fate. The fall of the harpoon does not, although it secures, always kill the animal, which is despatched in such a case by gun-shot.

In the Popo language the manatee is called "Yingbin-yingbin," and in Yoruba "Ese." They are, I have been informed, caught in the dry season, and when the lagoon waters are not full—say, during the first half of the year. Although it is the rule that they reappear with young at the commencement of the rainy season, and retire to the sea on the subsidence of the waters.

The flesh of the manatee is much appreciated by the natives, resembling a combination of veal and pork.

During my stay at Lagos I asked specially that I should be informed when one was caught, and on one Sunday morning, the 4th March last, I was gratified. A manatee had been caught in a drift-seine near Ajedé, in Jebu country, about ten miles from the bar of the Lagos river and up the lagoon. The animal was drowned after entanglement in the meshes of the net. The length was 9 feet, breadth at shoulders 2 feet, girth at thickest part 5 feet 6 inches. At a distance of 3 feet from the end of the tail the girth was 4 feet, breadth of tail 2 feet, length of fin, which was 7 inches wide, was 14 inches; mouth was 8 inches wide, skin about 1¼ inches — no doubt the

Manatus Senegalensis, found in the West African rivers, ranging up to a length of 15 feet—Vogel's "Ajuh" from the Benueh (branch of Niger).

Harpoons, spears, and earthen pots of narrow mouth are also used. The pots are large clay vessels sunk by stones or pieces of broken pots placed inside. They are perforated and baited before they are sunk, when they are placed on the side so as to admit of easy entry of fish. If placed in deep water they are connected by a leading-string to a papyrus stalk or other branch from the overhanging bank. In shallow water the position is staked. Such traps are occasionally visited, which is done as quietly as possible, when the mouths are closed by means of a small calabash in possession of visitor, the contents being thus secured.

The devices as to killing fish when caught are primitive and cruel in our estimate. Canoes are generally supplied with short stout clubs used for pounding the life out of the fish. Large stones are in like manner used. Canoes are so easy to capsize that large fish, when hooked, are allowed to exhaust themselves, or are killed by thrusts of a spear from the canoe.

I remember in Lagos lagoon seeing a large fish hooked and dragged to the side of a one-handed canoe, from which the occupant was engaged in killing his find by repeated rams of the whole handle of his paddle down the throat and stomach of the poor fish.

Drift-nets are resorted to, but chiefly in still sea or fresh water, the suspending ropes being of grass or of some fibre and floated by small calabashes or pieces of bamboo or. wood.

An ingenious device for capture resorted to behind Axim is described as follows in the 'To the Gold Coast for Gold' :—

" Across a stick planted in the river bed a light piece of bamboo was tied, and at its further extremity was suspended a string carrying fish-hooks. Above these a broad piece of wood, suspended so as to be half in and half out of the water, acted as a float and spindle. Above this again were tied four large shells, so that when a fish is hooked the shells begin to jingle, and the fishermen hid in the bush, immediately rush out and rescue the fish.''

Fishing Lines—of Lagos Native manufacture—of pine-apple or other fibre.

Fishermen, as a rule, make their own lines of fibre or of imported thread. Ordinary pieces of stone are used frequently for sinking purposes when lead cannot be had. As anchors, stones are more frequently used than any other device, secured to the canoes by country-made rope of grass or fibre.

On my return to England in April last I bought, as the steamer lay at anchor off the Kroo coast, a canoe containing also a specimen of a native fishing-pot and a specimen of a scoop or bale. Any wooden vessel with a lid may be converted into a fish-pot by the natives. The specimen I secured is nothing more than an American lard or biscuit box.

Native scoops are used for baling out water, and compare with similar devices used by Indians and others elsewhere. Such implements are not invariably resorted to, however, on the West Coast of Africa, where the natives are very dexterous both with hands and feet. I have often seen them baling out a canoe in a most amusing manner with their feet—literally kicking out the water.

The Kroo canoe alluded to is meant to accommodate one, and is a sample of the "dug-out" so common and universally known.

Besides the means for capture previously described the natives of Africa, as elsewhere among aborigines and in tropical parts, resort to vegetable products for the purpose of stupefying and poisoning fish. I may mention the " Toatoa," used in O' Quahao, a country lying to the south-east of the Ashantee kingdom, of which it was, not many years back, a dependency. The juice of this product is described as " so sharp that it wounds the skin on which it falls." The " Efswe " is also used there, which, thrown in a pounded condition into the river, when comparatively still, or into small ponds or pools, is said to stun the fish. Of these I have not, so far, been able to secure complete botanical specimens with a view to their identity or classification. At a certain season of the year, the lagoon waters where they approach the mouths of rivers become quite green from the presence of some class of algæ, and during that time the natives hesitate to eat fresh fish, alleging that there is a danger of being poisoned.

Reference is frequently made to this practice in the works that have been from time to time written on parts of this interesting continent.

Messrs. Capello and Ivens, in their work 'From Benguela to Yacca,' testify, in addition to the abundance of fresh-water fish, to the use of a leguminous plant called, in the vicinity of the river Luando, a branch of the Cuanza, " T'chingando," which, from its poisonous properties, causes vertigo among the fish and ensures their ready capture. They also record that the leaves of the " Ulo," a vegetable bearing a yellow flower, are also greatly used on the Cuango : " thrown into the stream they intoxicate the fish to such a degree that the creatures are easily taken with the hand."

In his Paper on ' Indian Fish and Fishing,' Dr. Francis

Day also made mention of a similar practice, when he described among means of capture "the taking of fish by poisoning pools of water by milk bush, tobacco leaves, Indian hemp, and many poisonous kinds of jungle fruits. This is generally carried on during the dry seasons of the year, when the pools in the rivers are still and hardly any current exists. It is very easy to collect the poisons—throw them into a pool, and await the fish floating intoxicated to the surface. These fish are sold in the markets."

The practice I have alluded to is of such general interest as to persuade me to trouble you with the following particulars of like trees and shrubs used similarly in Africa, details of which I have extracted from Oliver's 'Flora of Tropical Africa.'

Tephrosia Vogelii, a shrub 8 to 10 feet high, its branches woody ; ascending, clothed with dense spreading ferruginous or yellowish silky lines : found in Upper Guinea, Sierra Leone, Fernando Po, Princes Island, Nile land—Unyoro, Lower Guinea—Golungo Celto, and Pungo Andongo, Mozambique district—Zambezi, and Zanzibar.

Often used, in fact, cultivated, like the allied *Tephrosia toxicaria* in America, for the purpose of throwing into ponds to stupefy fish, called "Igongo" on the Gaboon.

Milettia ferruginea, a large tree with firm terete ultimate branches clothed with fine short ferruginous silky tomentum. "Berebera" is the Abyssinian name of this handsome tree. The powdered seed is thrown into the water to stupefy fish.

Derris uliginosa, a wide-climbing shrub with firm glabrous terete woody branches. Found in Mozambique district, Zambezi land, banks of the Luabo, and in the Zambezi delta. Stem used, when beaten, as a fish poison, acting rapidly and effectively. Extends through Asia to North Australia, and also occurring in Madagascar.

Randia dumetorum, a stiff spinous shrub. Nile land, Mozambique district; occurs commonly in most parts of India, and extends to Ceylon, Hong Kong, and the Malay Archipelago. *R. Kraussii*, Harv., from Natal, appears to belong to this very variable species. The fruit is said to act as a fish poison.

Morelia Senegalensis, an evergreen shrub of 12 to 30 feet, often arborescent and producing aërial roots. Upper Guinea— Senegambia, Aboh, Sierra Leone, Nupe, Old Calabar river— Nile land, Djurland, Bongo land. Used to intoxicate fish.

In 'The Annals and Magazine of Natural History,' No. 117, Sept. 1867, there is a translation of a most interesting article on Venomous Fishes, by M. Auguste Duméril, brought about by the many instances of poisoning due to the use of certain fishes as food, and, as allusion is made therein to the custom in some countries "to cast noxious plants into the water in order to render the fisheries more rapid and abundant," I venture here to invite my hearers to a reference to the views therein expressed.

It is stated, and condemned, that the Indians bruise the fruits of the *Cocculus suberosus* and many shrubs of the same genus, confounded under the name *Coque du Levant.* " Mix them with a species of crab, and make them into pellets of the size of a cherry, which the animals take with great avidity. The effect is very immediate." Of such a practice it is said by M. Boullay on the subject : " Fish taken with the aid of such a bait putrefy very readily, and if not cooked or prepared immediately may become venomous." Doubt has been thrown on this by M. Duméril, who has advanced that the *Coque du Levant* is frequently employed in India in fisheries whose products are intended for consumption.

I would yet quote from this article : " A further example of the innocuousness of fishes subjected to certain poisonous plants is furnished by M. de Castelnau ('Voy. dans les parties centr. de l'Amér. du Sud.' 1855. Paris, pp. 6 & 7.) An extremely plentiful supply of fishes having been obtained on the great lake near the Rio Sarayacu, in the Missions of the Ucayale, by means of the poison residing in the stems of the Barbasco or Necklace wood (*Jacquinia armillaris*, Linn.), these, after rapidly undergoing the destructive influences of the plant, were eaten without ill effect ; and the natives even drank the waters of the lake with impunity."

As a foot note to the above quoted review appears a very useful list, by M. Mouchon, of plants which were then known to be employed as auxiliaries in the capture of fishes, subdivided under the headings : (1), Plants that are baneful in effect upon the human species, particularly if the precautions be not taken of well clearing and scraping the fish before preparing it for food ; (2), Plants that are not hurtful to man. The list includes some orders peculiar to tropical Africa, and does not embrace the plants which I have already mentioned, which will explain why I dwell so much on the article of Venomous Fishes, my object being to endeavour to help those, who may help their countrymen—I mean the more enlightened and educated in West Africa—in the cessation or avoidance of practices so much to be condemned, and with such a doubtful issue, and to warn them that such practices are liable also seriously to so affect fish as to bring about, even after curing, sad results.

Nothing can be so good or wholesome, in my experience, as fresh-fish diet with nutritious accompaniments, and I have had visible proofs of the fact in the appearance of the coast people as compared with those of the interior, who are almost altogether dependent on, and prefer, unwholesome and unsound fish.

I can here remember what fine-looking people the Katanus—to be referred to later—are in spite of the malarious place in which they live ; they were, on the whole, a fresh fish-eating people, having plenty of open air exercise and abundance of bathing.

I am given to understand that no special diseases show themselves among the coast fishing population. I may except the greater liability to craw-craw and Guinea worm on the part of those engaged in fresh and brackish water, owing to constant wading and passing through grass. On the contrary the sea fishermen are about the healthiest class, as elsewhere, from their healthy occupation, comparative cleanliness, in the way of abundant sea-bathing, fresh fish-food, and the sale of surplus catch resulting in enabling them to supply themselves with other forms of diet. Their suffering from exposure is nil ; then it will be remembered that natives are very fond of oiling their bodies, which would greatly assist in keeping up their temperature, and then do away with risk of chill, so promotive of fever and rheumatism in Africa.

From the nature and general condition of the fish used as food, as also in consequence of the preference held for fish in a state of semi-decomposition rather than when fresh and wholesome, one is induced to look around for the issue of some ill consequence. It is not within my intention or scope to advance any theories, but I may repeat that the natives of West Africa suffer, besides ordinarily, much from elephantiasis, leprosy, yaws, cutaneous diseases, and ulcerations of a low order. The primitive and defective system of curing, apart from the semi-putrid condition of

[33]   D 2

the fish food, must lose, in such a climate, its efficacy, and thus it may be presumed that deleterious effects can be traced to its imperfect or bad preservation, such as, say, of the "herring," which the natives on the coast and in the interior principally consume.

Dr. Clarke, who was Colonial Surgeon on the Gold Coast, and surgeon to the natives, in his medical report for 1858 has dwelt on the food question as follows :—

"Elephantiasis and Lepra (leprosy) in all its hideous forms prevail. The natives suppose it may be induced by drinking excessively of palm wine which has been mixed with the juice of the bamboo ; but it may, with much greater reason, be accounted for by an excess of fish diet. A very large proportion of those who were treated at the dispensary were afflicted with scrofulous disease, either in the form of ulcerations of the skin, glandular swellings of the neck, or disease of the bones. The cause of its prevalence, I feel assured, is clearly traceable to the crowded, ill-ventilated and generally foul condition of their houses and sleeping places. The walls of most of their dwellings are formed of clay, which are rarely if ever whitewashed. Most of the rooms are miserably small, damp, dark, and badly ventilated, especially those devoted to sleep. In their sleeping places the poorer classes, and many persons in better circumstances, keep all the dirty clothing not in wear either about their beds or hanging from the wall, scraps of food and putrid fish being strewed about or collected in corners. I have observed that the mortality among the natives is greatest at the commencement and termination of the rainy season, and hepatitis, diarrhœa, and dysentery are then most prevalent, these diseases being then frequently brought on by eating new corn, ground nuts, casada, and yams before they are sufficiently dry. The food of the mass chiefly consists of vegetables and fruits with fresh fish and dried fish in excess, often so highly ammoniacal as to be commonly known under the name of 'stink fish,' with land snails and land and sea-crabs. But their principal dish is composed of fish, and, when they have the means, of fish, fowl, or meat, stewed singly or together : palm-oil, freshly expressed from the nut, being always an important ingredient in it. This stew is made piquant and wholesome by the addition of salt, bitter tomatoes or ocroes, shallots, or, as substitute for the latter, the dried bark of a tree called ' Edooah Ahyew' (which resembles the onion in flavour and taste), and abundance of red peppers."

"Animal food is, however, seldom eaten, and even milk is rarely used by them."

Dr. Clarke has been supported later by the experience of Colonial Surgeon Jones, from whose report in the year 1867 I extract as follows :—

" One of the most frequent complaints of the native population is constipation, which I attribute to the fact of their living all the year round on 'Cankey' and semi-rotten fish, and to the fact of these people being restricted to this miserable diet I think in a great measure is due the frequency with which they suffer from ulcers of the extremities, particularly of a low, indolent character, which are very difficult to heal."

I have not met in the Colony with any views since expressed as opposed to such opinions, but the conclusions of these gentlemen were no doubt based on the large consumption of what has been already described as stinking fish, on which the people have mainly to rely (and which they seem to prefer at any season) during the rough weather on the coast of Africa, occurring in the months of May, June, July, and August.

Medical experience of note elsewhere, such as that of Dr. Gavin Milroy in the West Indies, accords with the conclusions of Messrs. Clarke and Jones on the subject of the baneful effects innutritious and semi-putrid fish food must have on the human system.

I can recall here (I trust my memory serves me right)

the chief reasons I got from a medical man in Norway for the existence on its West Coast of so much leprosy, viz., bad food—principally fish—exposure, scanty clothing, want of cleanliness. Dr. Gavin Milroy, in a conversation I had with him, supported these reasons, explaining further that, on inquiry on the subject, he was informed that some Norwegians of the lower orders prefer tainted to fresh fish.

Again, on the contrary, in the discussion of a case of recovery from leprosy, by Mr. Jonathan Hutchinson, reported in the 'Lancet,' Feb. 15th, 1879, it is reported that Sir Joseph Fayrer said that if "the eating of putrid and decomposing fish were a cause of leprosy, then the whole of the inhabitants of British Burmah and the Malayan peninsula ought to suffer from leprosy, for that was their most favoured food. But leprosy was almost unknown in these countries; whereas it abounds in the Himalayas, where, as Mr. Macnamara had stated, fish eating did not and could not prevail. . . . Certainly in India leprosy was not due to fish diet."

Whether the disease be due to fish eating, its importation, surrounding circumstances of social condition, exposure, innutritious diet, malarial prevalence, seaside localities, the bacillus, its introduction into the system through the medium of putrid food, or by mosquito bite, is beyond my unprofessional power to advance; in fact it would be presumptuous on my part to even risk an opinion. The question seems yet a moot one, and, with reference to the disease, Dr. Erasmus Wilson has advanced, I think, in 1881, that the question of cause "must still remain unsettled until further information is obtainable. A specific form of bacillus has recently been found in leprosy, the lymphatics being believed to be the channels of infection."

Recent researches, according to Drs. Fox in the 'Epitome

of Skin Diseases,' point in the direction of the existence of a special bacterium (*Bacillus lepræ*).

"To be or not to be, that is the question."

Here offers a grand opening for display of West African medical talent.

I am not prepared to dwell further on this part of my Paper, beyond recording that it has not, unfortunately, been my experience to find extended, with exceptions, to special diseases and their causes that attention and interest which science and humanity dictate.

It is interesting to note how curious it is that red pepper (chillis, the fruit of *Capsicum annuum*) is so generally used in malarial Africa and in other tropical countries. In this use West Africa stands prominent. It may be concluded that people in such countries are always more or less below par, especially in Africa (for such is my experience), and that stimulant is deemed needful, and resorted to. The pepper affords a powerful stimulant, and promotes further the digestion—whether with an ultimate satisfactory issue or not is another question—in countries such as West Africa, where the digestive power becomes considerably impaired.

Salt forms an essential factor to the health and contentment of the natives, and is only somewhat devoted towards the curing of fish, being principally used as a condiment. Odd to say, it is largely imported into West Africa, its manufacture from salt water by the natives receiving but scanty attention. Beyond a matter of interest and of astonishment, the mention of this industry, as compared with salt importation, is scarcely worthy of notice.

For the purpose of curing fish, salt is only used on the coast, and even there not altogether, when the catch is exceptionally plentiful, and the scarce season has to be provided for. Salt-cured fish during the "scarce season," is used on the coast-line, finds its way into the interior, but is not appreciated in either locality as is "stinking fish." In fact, I have satisfied myself that the aborigines really prefer the latter where a choice was allowed or could be made : and even where fresh is used, there is, if it be available, some of the other mixed up with it, for the purpose of "flavouring."

With reference to shrimp curing, I would continue by remarking that the same system applies to fish, more particularly to the herring, which abounds towards the end of the rainy season. The catch is at times so great that the people really do not take the trouble to attempt, even in their primitive fashion, to cure what they can, but after satisfying what they may estimate as their wants, throw away the surplus. Salt curing, I repeat, is somewhat resorted to, as is also "smoking," but both systems are imperfect, and suffice as to efficiency but for a time, after which the fish becomes semi-rotten. So pronounced and offensive is the smell arising from its general condition that fresh-cured fish is commonly spoken of as "stinking fish." Its stench will be universally acknowledged by those who know West Africa. I do not mean to imply that it is always bad, but my own travels in those parts support me when I say that I have seen carriers and interior people partaking of fish food unfit even for a dog.

Again, on the modes of curing employed by the Bongos, Schweinfurth relates—

" There are two methods which the Bongo employ to preserve the flesh of their fish. Table salt they cannot get, but they substitute what they obtain from ashes. They cut the fish through lengthwise, simply expose it to be dried in the sun, and afterwards hang it up to be fumigated in the clouds of smoke which fill their huts. Another way is to cut the fish up and dry it, and then to pound it all up in mortars until it is reduced to a jelly, which is rolled into balls about the size of the fist. These, with their high flavour, form a favourite ingredient in soups and sauces which are certainly wanting in all other aromatic condiments."

The sale of salt acts well as a barometer of the state of the inter-tribal relations of the interior. It is often used as currency or means of barter, showing its importance. With petty warfare proceeding in the interior—a normal condition of things—and with roads blocked, or rather trade routes obstructed, as a sequence, the trade in this much-coveted article is small as compared with its disposal in peaceful times. It can then be judged why the curing by salt of the interior fresh-water fish is out of the question, as also why, when fresh fish is not to be had, "stinking fish" becomes the staple commodity for the daily meal.

Here follows the value of salt imported into the Gold Coast Colony during the four years given :—

Year.	Value of salt imported. Gold Coast.	Value of salt imported. Lagos.
	£	£
1878	1670 13 1	4250 8 7
1879	3441 12 10	2840 19 1
1880	4079 4 6	5439 18 9
1881	1682 7 3	8037 2 5

Fiscal conditions on imports differ in our West African Possessions : some articles of food are allowed to enter free, whereas on others an *ad valorem* rate and salt-tax are levied.

Such impositions cannot at present be said to have the same effect as it is advanced the salt-tax has had in India, as to fish-curing, for such is the depravity of the human taste in West Africa—the inheritance of birth and training—as elsewhere, that at times, and most frequently, semi-putrid fish is preferred to any other. In my statement I am supported by the fact that there is no gradual increase in the taste of the people for foreign-cured fish.

In such a depraved taste the Negro is not an exception, for of Balasore, in Bengal—I here extract from Dr. Day's paper previously referred to—it is stated by the Collector that—

"Fish sold in the markets is so stale that no European would touch it, and most of it is putrid . . . The people in this district do not salt their fish, they dry it in the sun, and eat it when it is quite putrid. They like it in this way, and there is no reason why they should be interfered with."

Oysters.

Edible oysters are found in beds, on the rocks running out into the sea, which are uncovered at low tide, and on trees (mangrove). The trade in oysters is large, but chiefly, in fact altogether, confined to the coast, as its delicate nature, even when cured as the natives affect, does not admit of long keep.

The trees on which oysters are usually to be found in the tropics are of the mangrove family, the nature of which, with their aërial roots, admits of their growth in the flow of the oyster spat, which is thus at times in part intercepted, adheres, and develops into what is commonly spoken of as the tree-oyster. Mangrove oysters are not as much sought after as bed or rock oysters, although they are collected for the sake of their shells, for the purpose of conversion into lime.

Bed-oysters are more extensively sought after. A solitary canoe at anchor over oyster-beds may be seen at times with no occupant. He has dived with his basket, and grabs in the mud (so long as his breath will allow him to remain under) for his prey, until by such repeated efforts he succeeds in filling his canoe. Women are usually the buyers and subsequent retailers of such commodity. Rarely, except for European tastes, oysters are sold open, but in bulk with shell on. Such as are not disposed of fresh are cured similarly as are shrimps and fish.

The oyster season, although the mollusc may be taken at any time, may be viewed to extend, as far as the Gold Coast colony goes, over six months or so of each year, during the rainy season. Oyster collectors make yearly presents to the fetish-priests, to invoke and propitiate the god of fish.

There is a certain danger associated with this industry, for it has been known that persons concerned in the same have fallen victims to sharks and crocodiles. The collection of the raw material can be followed out by any man or woman. Odd to say, among the Yorubas, he who follows the oyster industry is considered as of the lowest grade of society. In the past such a man would be denied marriage in a family of position above his social estimate. Women go in for the collection of mangrove-oysters.

In West Africa man has competitors as fish destroyers, such as the crocodile, shark, ray, otter, porpoise, water snake, turtle, tortoise, birds, etc.

The West African rivers at their mouths, and up a certain distance, abound in sharks, which are the terror of the natives. They are found in greater numbers at some places as compared with others, but so far as I know their catch is not profitably, if at all, followed up. Sharks are eaten in Western Africa, as in many other tropical countries ; and when consumption at the time is not equal to available quantity, the surplus is sun-dried or smoked, being treated as are herrings and shrimps.

> " Scale of dragon, tooth of wolf ;
> Witches, mummy ; maw, and gulf,
> Of the ravin'd salt-sea shark."

Lagos bar is noted as a favourable resort for this sea monster; and of the river St. John's, in Liberia, Burton speaks that "it owns a bar as infamous as that of Lagos for surf and sharks."

Of the Dahomean coast, the beach has been often unworkable as regards landing and loading, as the canoemen (Fantees or Accras, commonly known as "Minas"), whenever (and it is of frequent occurrence) one of them falls a victim to a shark, have absconded from time to time in abject terror. From Cootenoo, for instance, it is not an unusual thing to have at Lagos runaway crews amounting to sixty or eighty men who have escaped by the beach. The same has happened frequently in the other direction from Whydah. I was led to believe early this year, before I left Africa, that these means of escape from their employers had been cut off by Dahomean guards at either end. Here the French commercial houses have tried with some success the drift-net ; they have also used dynamite devices for the promotion of confidence among their employés, rather than the effective system, if not of gradual clearance, at least of considerable thinning.

In view of the field presented, it is astonishing why sharks are not put to use as in Norway, where they are captured for their livers ; or as in India and China, where the fins form a very important article in trade, the people of the former country preparing from them, in addition to other extracts, gelatine.

In Norway some of the fish furnish livers weighing only from 25 to 30 lbs., while from others livers of 220 to 450 lbs. are obtained.

If one can conjecture from the effect a malarial climate, especially that of West Africa, has on the human liver, and can deduce that the shark is similarly affected—at least the unacclimatised itinerant—a good and big find might be anticipated.

It is said of Norway that the carcasses of sharks have been of late years brought ashore for the purpose of being manufactured into manure or guano. The mode of capture there is by means of line and hook baited with seal blubber or some other rancid and strong-smelling bait. The annual yield from this fishery amounts to from 8000 to 10,000 barrels of livers, worth 150,000 gulden. The oil of the shark obtained by steam heating is said to be extremely fine, and is used for purposes of illumination.

I am reminded here of the remark of one of my boatmen at Lagos (a Krooboy), in answer to my questioning him. I may preface what I am going to convey by saying that Krooboys view sharks as their natural enemy and legitimate game. His opinion of this monster was that "he be debil man. He good for chop (food). He chop Krooboy, and Krooboy chop him "—mutual obligations of a curious nature.

In support of the value of a shark fin industry I embody as follows :—

"At Kurrachee a large fishery is practised. Dr. Buist, writing in 1850, states that there are 15 large boats, with crews of 12 men each, constantly employed in this pursuit ; that the value of the fins sent to the market varies from 15,000 to 18,000 rupees : that one boat will sometimes capture at a draught as many as one hundred sharks of various sizes ; and that the total number of sharks captured during the year amounts probably to not less than 40,000. Large quantities are imported from the African coast and the Arabian Gulf, and various parts on the coasts of

India.   In the years 1845–46, 8770 cwt. of sharks' fins were exported from Bombay to China.

Rays—like to the *Aetobatis*—known in Fantee as *Tantray*, are to be plentifully found on the West Coast of Africa, in the Gulf of Guinea, towards the end of the year, and in company with shoals of small fish.   They are at times caught in the hand-nets.   Natives are much afraid of the attacks from this fish, as the caudal spine has been found to be poisonous, and has inflicted wounds which have proved fatal.   Such wounds can be, it is said, however, successfully treated, when handled in time, by the natives, who use for the purpose the powdered caudal spine of like fish, mixed, with certain leaves and herbs.

I have with me the caudal spine of a small sting-ray, which was removed from the side of a fisherman of Quittah, Gold Coast.   In lifting the fish into the canoe, it struck him, the spine remaining in the wound.   Six hours later the man was seen by one of the Colonial surgeons, when the wound presented a very discoloured, unhealthy appearance.   The man died six days later from empyœma caused by the wound.

Writing of the poison organs of certain fish, Dr. Günther has stated, " That such organs are found in the sting-rays, the tail of which is armed with one or more powerful barbed spines.   Although they lack a special organ secreting poison, or a canal in or on the spine by which the venomous fluid is conducted, the symptoms caused by a wound from the spine of a sting-ray are such as cannot be accounted for, merely by the mechanical laceration, the pain being intense, and the subsequent inflammation and swelling of the wounded part terminating not rarely in gangrene."   This fish is cured in the manner already described, is sold in the markets, and is considered a great delicacy. The tail is used as a whip.

The crocodile, known locally in some places as the "cayman," and commonly called "alligator," deserves a passing notice. Most of the West African rivers and lagoons are infested with them; they are worshipped fetishly as a god, and are the terror of many a village bordering on their watery haunts.

Children and women have been often carried off, and many a person has been maimed, especially in the early morning, as they visit rivers for water. On such occasions, while women are filling their calabashes or earthen pots, one of the number is often employed to frighten off the monster by throwing large stones into the water beyond their dipping companions.

The skin of the crocodile is converted into caps and bags by the natives, and the flesh is smoked and eaten.

" Eat a crocodile ! "

Stories are heard of the game " catch-catch " between this monster and persons, as also of the latter being chased on land by the former.

It is told of a fresh-water pond at Dix Cove, Gold Coast Colony, in which there was a crocodile of some twelve feet long, which always appeared at the bank at the call from the " Fetishmen " for its meal of fowl.

An amusing story has been told me in connection with the doings of a crocodile. It is no uncommon thing for one of them to transfer its habitat from the main lagoon to some inland pool or lake at a distance. On one such journey a crocodile mistook the route, and mounted a bamboo fence that had partially fallen, thus affording a convenient camp for observation, we shall say. This lean-to fence partly enclosed a compound, in which at the time there happened to be a policeman, who, inspired with the proper sense of his duty, rushed at the creaking fence, which he embraced, expecting to find a would-be burglar, instead of our friend the crocodile !

I suppose a crocodile, as any other creature, can refer to a constable to be put right on a question of locality !

It is commonly believed by some tribes that the " Fetishman," when he wants to do injury to a family, can convert himself into a crocodile, and as such perpetrate his credited evil intent by maiming or carrying off—

> " Beguiled as the mournful crocodile
> With sorrow snares relenting travellers."

Edible turtle are found in abundance, but are not, such is my individual experience, as a rule, in good condition, being poor.   They are caught in the circular hand-nets and speared, but are generally captured on the beach, where they come to lay their eggs.   The natives on moonlight nights watch for them, cut off their retreat, and, turning them over on their backs, thus secure them.

The Ascension Lakes, supplied, I understand, as above, are well known in the West and South African squadron, providing as they do a rich and appreciated out-put.   Why could not some of the many "salt ponds"* adjacent to the African coast line be similarly used as rearing waters, and another industry be developed therefrom, although I doubt the suitability of turtle soup as a tropical diet in a malarial country where the "fitful liver" has to be gently treated, and we have no aldermen.

Fishing Towns and Villages.

Fishing towns and villages, often well marked by the groves of cocoa-nut trees that surround them, are to be

* Brackish inlets or salt-water lakes.

found scattered along the sea-coast, and on the banks of rivers or of inland waters; some permanently occupied, others only temporary residences of convenience in pursuit of calling. Alongside these, sometimes at a distance, the fishing-canoes are hauled up and picketed.

Lake Dwellings.

Swiss lake dwellings and Scotch crannogs of the past have afforded, especially of late, considerable attraction, and on the subject, by way of comparative interest in like structures of the present time, I am reminded of the lake dwellings of certain tribes who surround or live on the sheet of water known as the Denham waters, lying behind the Dahomean sea-board, and the rivers that flow into it. As the male occupants are mainly fishermen, or fishermen and farmers combined, I do not hesitate to include in this paper some notes of my experience of them.

During my administrations of the Government of Lagos I paid several visits to these waters—in fact have steamed through the water streets of the towns and villages to which I refer—and had thus the opportunity of observing for myself the modes of life on which I would ask permission to briefly dwell. Interest in the subject will be perhaps enhanced when I mention that these waters have, I believe, given rise to diplomatic correspondence in consequence of the acceptance by the French of the protectorate of the kingdom of Porto Novo.

These tribes are the Kátanus, Esos, and Whemians, who have not fishing resorts erected for convenience, but occupy large native villages and towns built entirely out and over the water.

The question naturally suggests itself, what is the cause

[33]   E

for such a resort ? It is explained when I say that these tribes once formed part of the old kingdom of Dahomey, which was in the past split up by inter-tribal wars, and the weak were not driven to the wall, but literally into the water, where protection was sought from their more powerful fellow-countrymen—viz., from the ancestors of the present occupants of the Dahomean kingdom —the protection being ensured from a knowledge of the fact that it has been for some time conveniently contrary to the Dahomean fetish to cross water, at least in canoes.

Such towns or villages have each a floating population, varying, I may estimate, from two or three hundred souls to as many thousands.

The people are fine and healthy, and, as a rule, are very free from disease. I may say they suffer from "craw-craw" and guinea worm.

Their houses are built upon piles or stout straight branches of hard wood, of some 3 to 6 inches diameter, which are secured as supports by being worked under manual labour from canoes into the bottom some 3 or 4 feet. The upper ends are then secured by crosspieces of like nature, on which is worked a bamboo flooring two-thirds or a half of which is covered in by a house, the uprights of which are fixed first, and secured below the platform to the supporting piles. The roof frame is next made on the platform, then covered with grass or bamboo leaves and raised to its position, when it is secured by the tie. The remaining portion of flooring is used as a verandah, or rest aloft and is sometimes covered in or not, according to the wish of the owner. In the construction no nails are used.

Houses are in shape rectangular, sometimes conical, having in the latter case the appearance of floating bee-hives of large proportions

These people are not only fishermen, but are pastoral, especially the Whemians; and their relative monetary positions, and consequent social status, may be guessed by the general appearance of their houses, and by the stand of cattle to be seen in the pens adjoining their houses, built on piles over the water, as are the dwellings. The absence or shallowness of the water at some sites in the dry season admits of the cattle being allowed to wander on *terra firma*, in fact of the erection and repairs of dwelling houses; but fodder has to be brought by canoe to the less fortunate creatures that have to eke out an existence in such pens as are always surrounded by water, until such time as they are tethered and transported by canoe to the butcher.

The length of the piles depends on depth of water, and on the probable rise in the rainy season. I have seen houses built over water some two to three fathoms deep. Should there happen to be a higher rise than allowed for, which at times happens, when even the platform is covered, a temporary flooring is made in the roof, with a hole in its thatch as a door, over which the people have to reside until the water has subsided.

Habit, associated with still-existing dread, leans them to a preference of a continuance of such occupations, although the people cultivate farms and make oil on the adjoining lands.

Domestic animals among them are pigs, goats, sheep, cattle, dogs, etc.

The men fish, farm, and trade, while the women attend to the live stock and attend markets, paddling their own way; they also fish.

The fishing gear is similar to what I have already described.

[33]

Inter tribal fighting, whether for offence or defence, has been conducted from canoes capable of holding two or three persons, their weapons being guns, harpoons, spears, and clubs. So uncertain are they of safety, and so apprehensive of danger, that they keep, when travelling, secured against the sides of the canoes, guns and a quantity of ammunition. Their beds are similar to what is usually enjoyed even on land, viz., a reed or fibre mat, on the bare floor.

Polygamy exists, but wives and children live in separate houses from husbands. On invitation a particular wife will join her husband, and on such occasion, generally at night, paddle her own canoe to him, and convey—the rule—his evening meal.

Having now dealt as far as space will allow me with the coast line, I will refer to the islands.

Canary Islands.

I know of only two systematically and profitably pursued industries on this coast to which I would make allusion in this Paper, viz., the "cod and bream" fishery of the Canaries, and the whaling of the African Atlantic.

Of the former, the fishing-ground may be considered as lying between the Canaries, Cape Verde islands, and like latitudes on the African coast, or from $14°$ or $15°$ to $32°$ or $33°$ N. lat., the favourite site being between the island of Fuerto Ventura, Cape Bojador, and Cape Blanco.

Much attention has of late been directed to these waters, and a source of considerable wealth no doubt presents itself. It has been advanced—an open question—that there is more fish between these islands than around the coasts of Newfoundland. M. Berthelot, in a work on the Canary fishery, came to the conclusion that the quantity of fish caught by one man in the Canaries is equal to that caught by twenty-six in Newfoundland. These advances furnish just ground for argument into which I do not intend to enter here.

The class of vessel employed is represented by the fore-and-aft schooner of varying size, from 20 to 50 tons, with a crew each of from 18 to 40 men and boys. In the years 1879 and 1880, the craft employed in this trade numbered 31 vessels, with a total of 913 tons, of which 16 belonged to the island of Grand Canary, and 15 to the island of Lanzarote.

Fishing-boats work all the year; but the season for the African coasts is given as from April to September, distinct, it would seem, from the island season mentioned as between September and March.

Fish are caught by hook, but from Grand Canary nets are also used. A system prevails of trailing a number of hooks attached to lines run out at right angles to the vessel, representing a means of capture that shows at times a good return.

The curing is done by salting, which is effected on board the schooners; but the imperfect process has been advanced as a reason why there has not been a greater development of the industry, and more appreciation of the cured fish. Another consequent industry has sprung up, viz., schooner-building in the island of Grand Canary.

The following is a list extracted from Consul Dundas' report, in 1877, on these islands, of the principal fish, ranging in weight from 15 lbs. to 65 lbs. each, included in what I may call the Grand Canary and Lanzarote fish industry :—

"Cherna or Cherne (*Perca cernua*), similar to cod, and considered inferior to Newfoundland cod.

Sama (*Serranus acutirostris*), very common, large excellent fish ; fished for in the arm of the sea that separates Grand Canary from the coast of Africa.

Sama Dorada (*Dentex vulgaris*).

Sama Grande (*Chrysophrys cæruleosticta*), weight rarely passes 45 lbs.

Sama (*Dentex filosus* and the *Pagrus auriga*).

Corbina (*Corvina nigra*), weight 30 lbs. to 45 lbs. ; fished for in the channel separating the archipelago of the Canaries from the African coast.

Bosinegro (*Pagrus vulgaris*).

Abadejo (*Serranus fuscus*).

Pez-rey (*Temnodon saltator*), average weight 20 lbs. ; very plentiful about Fuerte Ventura.

Rubio (*Trigla lineata*).

There is another species of Abadejo, which at Lanzarote and Grand Canary goes by the name of Abriote, of which the flesh is said to be excellent. It is met with in immense numbers on the African coast, and attains a large size, weighing as much as 30 lbs. Finally, a fish locally called Tasarte, said to be very like salmon. These are the kinds caught in greatest abundance by the men employed in the craft."

Large supplies of salt fish are exported for Cuba, but statistics are not obtainable as to quantity or value.

Consul Dundas has stated that ordinarily 40 tons may be loaded in three days. Other estimates give the catch per vessel per diem at from 15 to 39 quintals of 200 lbs. each.

The average amount of fish caught during 1880 by the vessels of Grand Canary, has been returned as 1,414,000 kilos., of which 1,122,000 kilos. were salted :—

Value of fish	. . . .	£33,208
,, nets used	. . . .	£5,292
,, 22 vessels with 740 tons	. . . .	£14,250

with 1,190 as the number of men employed in the industry.

Within 1880 and 1881 a French company has been sending steamers to Cape Blanco to purchase fish from the island vessels, which was conveyed for sale fresh to Marseilles. I am led to believe that this enterprise has failed, the refrigerating process not proving equal to the want. It has been said that the fish, on arrival at Marseilles, often proved unfit for food, and when even fit, did not admit of farther transport, both on account of condition and expense.

A considerable number of American ships, nearly all whalers, resort to Grand Canary for the purpose of obtaining supplies of provisions, water, and coal. It is, besides, known that there is often a whale-run in the vicinity of these islands, especially between Teneriffe and Grand Canary, and that from Santa Cruz (capital of former) anchorage, the American whalers often pursue, within one or two days' sail; indeed are at times engaged in whale fishery within sight of the islands.

It will be in place here to mention, that in 1880 there were 111 vessels engaged in the whale-fishing on the North and South Atlantic grounds, whence oil and bone were taken worth 908,771 dollars. Mr. Brown Goode has, however, stated that, "the whale fishery has of late years greatly decreased in value, owing to the introduction of mineral oils, and the great diminution in the number of whales—due to over fishing."

Some further particulars on this industry will be found in my remarks on St. Helena.

The development of a large fish industry under the name of the "Canario-African Fisheries Company," began some two and a-half years ago, and conducted by the energy and experience of Signor Silva de Ferro, proceeds from the Island of Gracioza to the north of Lanzarote of the Canaries. The working fleet is composed of two steamers of 50 tons each, engaged in transporting clean fish from the banks to Gracioza at eighty tons a week; six schooners of some 60 or 70 tons each, and ten sea-fishing boats (the schooners and boats conduct the fishing on the banks).

The industry is pursued all the year round, and carried on south of Canaries along the African coast, as far as Cape Blanco, viz., between 29° and 20° N. lat. Pelagic and shore fish are most plentiful, and offer here as elsewhere on this coast a field for an extended industry.

Signor Ferro has assured me, that within fifteen minutes he had on one occasion secured from the African shore 20 tons of herrings by means of a seine of 90 fathoms in length, let down by one small boat; further, he has seen one of his Masters catch in 32 fathoms of water—depth at which fishing for big fish is generally conducted—110 large fish within two hours.

Within four months, 600 tons of dry and pickled fish have been exported from Gracioza, where the air is said to be so dry that the cleaning, pickling, and drying process only requires ten days, when the fish, sometimes two or three inches thick in the meat, is ready for export. The directions of export have been to Spain, Cuba, South America, and Fernando Po, the transport being effected by sailing vessels, and steamers.

Signor Ferro can load now in ten days what used to take formerly two months. This saving of time is due to the use of herring—so easily and generally obtained—as bait. Formerly the Canary fishermen, who are described as so conservative as not to have made any progress, at least, in this industry, for centuries, had to purchase the octopus —to be found only at certain places—from the Moors on the African coast, and with it fish for "chopa," a sea-bream which represented their bait for the large fish.

As an encouragement, considerable land concessions on the Gracioza Island were made by the Spanish Government, in the first instance to Signor Ferro, who has transferred his rights to the above-named company, which command the whole of one side of the harbour lying between Gracioza and Lanzarote, represented as the only safe and commodious anchorage amongst the islands or on the neighbouring African coast, before River Ouro, where the peninsula forming this harbour of refuge for fishing craft has been purchased in the Spanish interest from the Moors by the Company.

It has been represented to me that nine-tenths of the inhabitants of the Canaries and Cape Verde, live on fish with their toasted corn or flour—"Gofio"—and on my inquiries as to the existence of leprosy, I am informed that the "fishermen are very subject to sores and ulcers of a very permanent description."

Red coral and sponge are to be found around Gracioza.

In view of the opening presented for the growth of a fish-oil, and guano trade, it does seem surprising to find guano, and chemicals for the manufacture of guano, among the imports into the Canaries. What has been in the past done, or is being done, with its surplus fish or its offal ?

I am glad to find that the eyes of the Canario-African Fisheries Company have been opened to a similar view as have mine, and that fish-oil and guano industries are likely to grow up.

With reference to the other Spanish Possessions, Fernando, Annobon, Elobey, Coresco, San Juan, etc., with a given population of 35,000, the natives follow a like primitive fish industry as is to be found elsewhere among their fellow-countrymen along the coast.

It becomes here my duty to warn speculators against the Canary Quarantine Laws, which in their operation are very fitful. They say that, on one occasion, because cholera was in Egypt or in India, the authorities of the Islands deemed it prudent to enforce their sanitary precautions against their own fishing vessels, because they had been engaged on the West African banks.

There is also a very good story told in connection with this subject, which must have got about also when some Asiatic epidemic was more heard of than usual.

While the channel fleet of six ships lay once at Grand Canary, a mail steamer arrived from the West Coast of Africa. The Admiral of the Fleet caused her to be visited, with a view to securing a grey parrot. The master of the steamer sent back word to the effect that, while he was sorry he had no parrots for sale, yet, if the Admiral would accept, he would be happy to give him one. The latter was condescending, and caused to be sent the " dingy " for the parrot. As the steamer had not at the time received " pratique," the boat was taken under her bows, and the parrot in cage was lowered by a rope into the stern-sheets of the " dingy." At the moment, which proved afterwards awkward, the local official who was keeping guard around the mail steamer appeared, and, on inquiry into the case, declared that if the parrot were taken to the flagship the squadron would be placed in quarantine, and if even the parrot were returned to the steamer, the result would be the same when the " dingy " got back to her station.

The parrot was eventually taken alongside the flagship,

the guard-boat escorting the dingy ; and on the matter
being reported to the Admiral, he ordered H.M.S. "Dingy"
to be anchored in the line in her station as seventh ship,
and, on this being done, the fleet were informed that the
dingy had taken Fleet No. 7 ; next that No. 7 was in
quarantine, and that the remaining ships were not to com-
municate with her.

So the poor "dingy," with her crew, inclusive of parrot,
remained anchored in discomfort, but in importance, while
a large yellow flag floated over her bows, until—well,
nothing further has been logged.

Cape Verde Islands.

According to the census of 1878, the Cape Verde islands,
ten in number, situated about 320 miles from the coast of
Africa, contained a population of 99,318. In 1881 the
British subjects were 89.

The growing importance of St. Vincent as a coaling
station is well known.

Although the manufacture of salt forms an important
industry in some of the islands, yet the absence of protected anchorages has no doubt interfered with the development of a fish industry. From the remarks on the
Canaries it will be gathered that the fishing grounds of
the Cape Verde islands are worked by vessels of the
former archipelago.

It is stated of the coral, that although "considerable
quantities of good quality are found in the neighbourhood
of the islands, nevertheless the Portuguese inhabitants
appear to take but little interest in this remunerative
business, and the fisheries are entirely conducted by Italian
and Spanish firms."

The value of coral obtained in 1879 equalled 18,061,840 reis, viz., £180,618.

To the other Portuguese possessions on this coast, viz., at Senegambia and Bissao, with a population (1873) of 9282, Princes and St. Thomas Islands with a population (1879) of 20,931, Ajuda (Whydah) with a population (1873) of 4500, and Angola, Ambriz, Benguela, and Mossamedes, with an estimated people of 2,000,000, the allusion *in re* the Cape Verdes to the non-existence of a developed fish industry beyond the primitive native calling will, I am led to believe, equally apply.

St. Helena.

The population of St. Helena has been returned for 1881 as 5,059, of whom 4,511 are given as natives. There were 171 boatmen and fishermen.

In Mellis's "St. Helena" will be found the following description of the fishermen:—

"Those men who prefer exclusively to follow the noble calling of fishermen number about 80 or 90, but they are a class who through years past have lived away from civilization : their wives and children occupying small miserable huts, or nearly inaccessible caves along the rocky shores, where they are altogether far removed, partly through their occupation, and partly through their long-acquired habits of indolence and demoralisation, from any beneficial influences. The men themselves, although there are some few exceptions, are for the most part satisfied to bring in just sufficient fish as will afford food and obtain a supply of Cape wine for a few days, when, after indulging in the excess in the latter, and recovering from their half stupefied state, they proceed out again for the same purpose."

There are no fresh-water fishes indigenous to the island, due, no doubt, to its volcanic nature. Albecore, barracouta and mackerel constitute the chief food of the population.

The fish field, which is represented as bountiful, is regarded with indifference. Although the fishermen have comparatively no bad weather to encounter, there is really no system of fishing or fishing trade. " Beyond a very partial and scanty contribution to the supply of food for the inhabitants, no use," according to the above-quoted author, "is made of the fish, or profits derived from it."

St. Helena and its surrounding sea offer a grand opening of economic importance for a large fish industry which might rival that of the Cape Colony.

The small amount of fishing carried on is with hook and line, either from the shore or from small rowing boats, which do not venture far out from the island.

The values of imports for 1880 and 1881 are returned as £54,272 and £53,169, and include £37 and £78 on account of imported fish, and £55 and £64 on account of intro-duced salt.

It is as well to know that St. Helena seems to be resorted to as the depôt for the American whale industry of the South Atlantic and more southern seas.

The Blue Books for the island show that there were imported by American whalers, and exported in American ships for the U.S., in 1879, 1880, and 1881, connected with this trade, bone and oil to the returned value of £32,190, £50,730, and £27,680.

In a most useful map of the world, prepared by the United States, and courteously placed at my disposal for the present occasion, there will be seen the extent and dis-tribution of the present and abandoned American whaling grounds.

The sites which may be perhaps considered as of this paper lie approximately within 30° W. and 20° E. long., and 20° N. and 40° S. lat. The area may be estimated by the bounding degrees of Lat. and Long., and is made up of the "Cape Verde," * "Ascension † and St. Helena," ‡ "West and South African," § and "African Atlantic" grounds.

While on this subject I may record the following description by the owner, Signor Ferro, of a fishing net in his possession of West African manufacture, made of the sinews of the whale, so far as one can presently judge without seeing it, as among the Cape Flattery Indians and Eskimos of North America.

"As to the net, it was brought from the Arabs of the Rio de Oro (River Ouro) ; it is some thirty fathoms long and one and a half fathoms deep, and of one inch mesh. It has the appearance of being made of thick guitar strings, but the Arabs explained that they made it from the intestines of a whale which stranded on the coast. The net is made without the help of either a netting needle or gunge ; they tied each knot with their fingers, twisting at the same time the cord as required. Notwithstanding this laborious way of making it, the net is perfectly regular throughout. The knot used is the same as used here, which they learnt from the fishermen (of Canary). It is weighted at the bottom by round beads of red earthenware of their own manufacture, about one inch in diameter. The corks are the same size and shape as the leads (?), and made from pieces thrown up upon the shore."

* 22° N. ; 15° N. Lat. from West African shore to 30° W. Long.
† 5° and 25° S. Lat. ; 3° and 10° W. Long.
‡ 5° N. Lat. and 38° S. Lat. ; average breadth between 5° and 20° E. Long.
§ 30° and 40° S. Lat. ; 10° E. and 25° W. Lon

There are certain local taxes under Ordinance No. 2 of 1868, which may be viewed as telling indirectly against the fish industry. I allude to the licence of fishing boats, whale boats, etc. There are no customs dues on imported fish or on salt.

Coral is remarkable for its absence, one species (*Phymactis*) being found on the coast, and two or three kinds in the surrounding seas.

————————

With the means lying at their very door, I may say— viz., the fish, which in other countries would be, and is, turned to profitable account of considerable proportion—the inhabitants of West Africa, including her archipelagoes, are, from the want of education—may be from other additional causes—regardless of it. An industry, true, is pursued but not with the energy the field deserves.

An extensive sea-shore, rivers, and lagoons ; streams and inlets to permit of ascent of spawning fish ; absence of manufactories to pollute waters ; little traffic disturbance of the waters, present perhaps favourable conditions for the development of a large and wholesome fish trade.

Against the migration of fish however we have the action of almost a constant thundering surf in the Gulf of Guinea, and we must not forget the cataracts so often met during the dry season in West African rivers ; they are however covered with water in the " rains," and then should offer little obstacle.

Sufficient, I am sure, has been advanced in support of the fact that there is an abundance of fish.

It would seem to me that the herring, for instance, offers an industrial opening that should prove remunerative.

Professor G. Brown Goode, in his report (1877) on the American menhaden, has stated :

"Again, on the West Coast of Africa occurs a species, *Brevoortia dorsalis*, closely resembling the menhaden. An old fisherman of Maine told me that he had seen the menhaden in immense quantities on the West Coast of Africa, where the negroes spear them and eat them."

Why should there not be a West African "Menhaden" fishery of some dimensions ? Not much more than twenty years ago the American menhaden fisheries were of very small importance, and the business of the manufacture of oil and guano in its infancy. See what gigantic strides this industry has taken, and the proportions and importance it has assumed!

The plant, free from complication, for making oil and guano, on a small scale as an experiment, need not cost more than £30 or £40. The process of manufacture seems simple in the extreme, viz., boiling the fish, skimming off the floating oil, pressing (for more oil) and drying the refuse which represents the guano ; there has to be also, I believe, a certain clarification of the expressed oil.

Hulks anchored outside the naval regulation distance from shore—I think three miles, so as to avoid, it is said, the effects of malaria—and thus beyond the action of the surf, might be resorted to as floating oil-factories, with the requisite supply, for fishing purposes, of hands, canoes and boats, and improved gear, to be worked as to fishermen by Krooboys or canoemen of other tribes. The industry might be associated with existing mercantile undertakings, perhaps through the medium or under the superintendence of the Masters of the many trading vessels that are to be found so long at one time on the coast. The small local steamers could be used during the slack trade time, if the herring season suited, in increasing the catch.

This Paper must, I would deign to hope, be therefore viewed, not as a scientific venture, nor yet as the exponent of any theories—for other demands on my time have not admitted of my following up, as closely as I should have wished, fish as a study—but rather as a convenient collection of gleanings from and references to other works bearing on the subject, and the record of my own experience.

I must acknowledge its incompleteness and imperfection, but console myself with the hope that it contains information which may have escaped others either in reading or in observation, and may form a groundwork for later, if not correction, at least elaboration and study on the part of those who can spare the time to the subject, and thus prove to be the means of attracting increased attention to that interesting and not "Expiring continent," with an ultimate issue of beneficial results, whether in the shape of addition to fish or other industries—a grand opening—or in a humanitarian sense of a more full and healthy food supply, and of consequent indirect benefit to the well-being of our People in Africa.

Yet, while I confess that this task might have fallen to better and more able hands, I will not give way in the sense of pleasure I have felt in undertaking it, feeling that it is the bounden duty of every one to promote, as far as his lights may admit, whether directly or indirectly, the condition of the people among whom his lot may be cast.

The Missionaries, in all the ramifications of their work, the Mercantile World, outside the circle of Government officials, represent means of contribution of material towards increased scientific knowledge, and it is to be hoped that an allusion to their importance as Agents in such a way may bring about fruit. West Africa however affords at present in our Possessions no magnets for the growth of scientific attraction and interest in the shape of Museums, Botanic Gardens, Herbariums or Model Farms, wants deeply felt in justice, if not to more, to its fauna and flora.

·The climate of West Africa may not admit of general colonisation, nor should it be necessary, for it offers good material for development ; while acknowledging it is bad, and, although such, has been often painted in the worst colours, yet it will continue to admit of the further import of commercial enterprise, resulting in more good to its undertakers and to Her People.

In the preparation of this Paper I am indebted to the courtesy and attention of many, especially to Dr. Günther of the British Museum, and to Dr. Murie of the Linnean Society, and I trust that this brief acknowledgment of my debt may be generally accepted.

DISCUSSION.

Mr. EDWARD JEX said the capture of barracouta and bonito on the coast of Guinea had been mentioned, but no mention was made of the manner in which they were caught ; the same with regard to the herring and mackerel.

Captain MOLONEY said the barracouta and bonito were caught with hook and line, the herring and mackerel were caught with a circular hand-net, which, perhaps, in its closing action by weighted edge and result, might bear some slight comparison with the purse-seine net, but for a detailed description he would beg leave to refer Mr. Jex to page 24 of his Paper, and to the miniature model before the Conference.

Captain J. D. CURTIS said he had had considerable experience on the West Coast of Africa, including the Gold Coast; with regard to the fishing, it appeared to be *nil* on the Gold Coast, for he had had the misfortune to cruise up and down there for nine months, in 1851 and 1852, and never fell in with any fishing canoe. An old messmate of his told him that in 1845 or 1848 one of the commanders there used occasionally to throw over a trawl from the brig, with which they caught sole and turbot, which, after supplying the sick, were divided between the officers and crew. On the West Coast the fish caught in the trawl were mullet, bream, and red fish, called snapper. At Loando they caught what were called snappers, or sea bream, in about sixty fathoms water, and in Elephant Bay there was abundance of grey mullet. In the Portuguese Settlements fishing was carried on by cabbage wood rafts and canoes, and there was a large establishment in Little Fish Bay for drying fish; they dried in eight or nine days in the sun, but unfortunately the wind carried the sand over them, and made them rather gritty. At Ambrizette a peculiar small double canoe is used. If the Commission could impress on the Admiralty the desirability of each ship carrying a trawl as well as the seine, there was no doubt a great deal of fish could be caught, which would be very advantageous to the crews, but unfortunately many captains used to think more of their paint than anything else, and objected to fishing. He recollected on one occasion seven porpoises were harpooned in one watch. When off Lagos, a quantity of condemned pork being thrown overboard, the next day a number of large sharks were caught—not like the Arctic shark. He had no doubt wherever there was a sandy bottom fish would be found, especially at rivers' mouths. With regard to the turtles at the Ascension, they came up to lay their eggs ; on their return men employed for the purpose captured them, and deposited them in the turtle ponds for use when required. They were served out as fresh-meat rations twice a week : the small ones when hatched found their way to the sea. The pond is only a depôt for keeping them ; they did not breed there at all. There is a peculiar turtle found in the mouth of the Congo with a head somewhat resembling a bat's. I have not seen the kind anywhere else. Barracouta, porpoises, bonito, dolphin, sucker-fish, pilot or zebra fish, cat-fish, and pouter-fish are to be found on the Gold Coast : off the Congo, whales, thresher, sword-fish, and saw-fish. A saw-fish cut my boat's cable, a $3\frac{1}{2}$-inch hawser, in two ; a friend of mine had· a similar misfortune off Cabenda.

Mr. JEX had been pleased to hear the remarks of Captain Curtis, showing that there were bottom fish on the coast of Africa, the Paper being mostly devoted to surface swimming or round fish.

Mr. BANDFORD GRIFFITH said he had been up and down the coast three or four times, and although twenty years ago there must have been no fishing, there were now fishing boats to be seen at all places. At Sierra Leone they came and offered fish for sale ; and lower down, on the Liberia coast and at Axim, he had seen numbers of fish on shore, but they were all sharks, varying in length from one to twenty-four feet. A little above Axim there were great numbers of sword-fish, and off the Dahomean coast he had seen sword-fish twelve or fourteen feet long. At Accra he had seen fishing boats going out morning after morning and coming back in the evening ; and at Lagos there were regular fishing villages, though there the fishermen did not go out beyond the surf. No doubt one reason why Captain Moloney had not referred to bottom fish was, that the people on the part of the coast he had principally dealt with rarely went out to sea, but fished chiefly in the lagoons, or within a few miles of the coast ; they did not as a rule get deep-sea fish, nor in fact did they endeavour to catch large fish, for they might very often meet with sharks, which were very troublesome customers. They were much indebted to Captain Moloney for having produced such an interesting Paper with such small material available.

Captain CURTIS said it might be worth noting that on one occasion he recollected capturing a porpoise which had a squid inside of it.

Mr. SAVILLE KENT then proposed a vote of thanks to Captain Moloney. He must say that the impression on his own mind was that, if this Paper had not been read, there would have been a considerable gap left in the literature of the Exhibition ; and they were also indebted to him for the illustrations which accompanied it. He hoped Captain Moloney would not feel that the apparent paucity of numbers was any indication of the interest felt in the Conference. He was glad to see that there were present representatives from China, Japan, the Australian Colonies, and North America, which was a more correct indication of the extent of interest taken in this Paper.

Mr. BLOOMFIELD, in seconding the motion, said they had been favoured with some remarks by a gentleman who had also been on the coast of Africa, and knew something of fishing there, but unfortunately it appeared he had been under the command of gentlemen who were not particularly favourable to that occupation. Still it appeared that they had nothing to do but throw overboard something or other, and the fish were caught, and the sick were benefited. He had, however, been able to add to the list of fish known on that coast some of which were not represented in the Exhibition. A remark was made in the Paper with reference to there not being aldermen on a certain portion of the coast where there were plenty of turtles. Of course aldermen were entitled to eat turtles, and very few other people could afford it; but, on the other hand, there was a large community not far off which at the present moment were prevented apparently by the aldermen from eating something which was a great deal cheaper than turtles. Herrings, mackerel, and all sorts of fish, might be cheaper at the present moment if an opportunity were given by certain aldermen to have those fish brought into a central market with greater facilities, so as to afford sustenance to the poor. He hoped the remarks made from time to time with reference to that point would receive the same careful attention on the part of the public which other subjects had already received. The places now described were a long distance off, but those present yesterday would remember that the gentleman from Japan had produced what looked more like a lump of stick than anything else, which was in reality a fish, so preserved as to be capable of being transported all over the world, and kept for any time, and yet it could easily be converted into a pleasant and valuable article of food. Not a Paper had been read at these Conferences but showed more or less that, however the population might increase, there would be found in every part of the globe where the flag of Great Britain floated a source of supply for the national wants, though but for this great Fisheries Exhibition a deal of this information would not have been forthcoming. He therefore considered that those gentlemen who came forward to read these Papers were entitled to the thanks not only of those who heard them, but of the country at large, and, in fact, of the whole civilised world.

Mr. JEX said there were thousands in the City of London besides aldermen who ate turtle ; and as to stopping the fish coming to the great centres of England, it was not the aldermen but the railway carriers who were the obstacles. A gentleman wrote to him from Glasgow that he could pay the freight of a barrel of herrings to Sidney and back and have a surplus left. It was not a question of the aldermen, but of the railway ring, and he hoped the Railway Commissioners would take the matter in hand and put a stop to the heavy charges now imposed for the carriage of fish, and thus enable him to bring fish not only from Scotland but from the west coast of Ireland, where there was an immense supply.

Mr. OKOSHI said there was no doubt that this Paper had thrown great light on the fisheries of Africa. The Japanese were a great fish-eating people, and in fact a great portion of them lived on fish ; they not only ate fish which were commonly used here, but some other kinds, as the octopus ; and as he found from the Paper that the fish was caught in the Canary Islands, he should like to know whether it was used there as food, as it was in Japan and China. It might seem curious to Englishmen that this fish should be eaten, but he could assure them it was really very delicate.

The vote of thanks having been carried unanimously,

Captain MOLONEY, in responding, said that he had already sufficiently trespassed on the generous patience of Sir Ambrose Shea and of the audience, and therefore would be brief. It did not require, fortunately, many words to convey his appreciative acknowledgments of the terms of the vote of thanks that had been so flatteringly pronounced by Mr. Saville Kent, and of the manner in which it had been received.

In the preparation of the Paper which he had just read, he had simply done his duty by the Exhibition, but more particularly by the people amongst whom he had the honour of serving for some years. The Pamphlet might be accepted as the record of so much information in a convenient form as may have escaped others either in reading or in observation, and may prove to be the groundwork for later study and increased attraction with an outcome, he hoped, of beneficial results, whether in the way of an increase to our industries or, humanitarianly speaking, of a healthier food supply.

As to the native fishing industry in the Bights of Benin, Gold Coast, and off West Africa, Captain Curtis would be gratified to know that it had considerably increased since the time—over thirty years ago—of which he had spoken ; and, in view of such a fact, Captain Moloney did not deem it necessary to modify in any way the particulars of his Paper.

Whilst thanking Captain Curtis for the further information, as regards Ascension, for which the Conference were indebted to his experience, Captain Moloney added that he had been fortunate enough at times, whilst in the Administration of the Government of Lagos, to receive from different commanders of Her Majesty's ships very fine turtle transported from the island of Ascension, where in the ponds or lakes, which were fed as previously described, he was given to believe a considerable rearing turtle industry proceeded for the benefit of the local squadron and for others, among whom he was glad to find himself numbered occasionally.

As regards the reference to the octopus, to which atten-

tion had been invited by Mr. Okoshi, he did not allude to
its catch as a later economic food industry ; it was simply
caught off the coast of Western Africa, to be used as bait.

Mr. HOUNSELL then proposed a vote of thanks to the
Chairman, who had occupied the platform three times that
day. It was not necessary to say anything in support of
the resolution, but he could not pass a higher encomium on
the Chairman than by saying, what he said most cordially
of himself that morning, that if at any time he could assist
the work of the Exhibition by doing anything in its favour,
it was a pleasure to him.

Mr. JEX seconded the motion, which was carried unanimously.

The CHAIRMAN said it was to him a very grateful duty
to have had the opportunity of assisting in any way the
object for which the Exhibition was established.

List of Memoirs dealing specially with the Crustacean-Fauna of the West Coast of Africa (North of Tropic of Capricorn) and the Islands of the same sub-region—for which I am indebted to Mr. E. J. Miers, of the British (Natural History) Museum.

Studer, Th.—Verzeichniss der Crustaceen, welche während der Reise S. M. S. Gazelle an der West - Kuste von Africa, Ascension, und der Cap der Guten Hoffnung gesammelt wurden.   pp. 1–32, pls. i., ii.   Berlin, 1883.   4to.

E. J. Miers.—On a collection of Crustacea made by Baron H. Maltzan at Goree Islands, Senegambia.   Annals and Mag. of Nat. Hist. (ser. 5) viii.   pp. 204–220, 259–281, 364–377. pls. xiii.-xvi.   (1881.)

Dr. A. G. Günther.—On a collection of Crustacea made by Mr. T. Coury in Ascension Island (*crustacea by E. J. Miers*). Annals and Mag. of Nat. Hist. (ser. 5) viii.   pp. 432–434. (1881.)

A. M. Edwards.—"Description de quelques espèces nouvelles de Crustacés provenant du Voyage aux Iles du Cap Vert de Mdlle. Bouvier et de Cessac."   Bulletin de la Société Philomathique de Paris.   pp. 3–13.   (1878.)

Crustacea by *C. Spence Bate*, F.R.S., in the work on St. Helena by J. C. Melliss.   London.   8vo.   1875.

A. Milne-Edwards.—"Description de quelques espèces nouvelles de Crustacés provenant du Voyage de M. A. Bouvier aux Iles du Cap Vert."   Revue et Magasin de Zoologie, pp. 350–355, 374–378, 409–412.   (1869.)

A. Milne-Edwards.—"Observations sur la Faune carcinologique des Iles du Cap Vert."   Nouvelles Archives du Muséum. pp. 49–60, pls. 16–18.   (1868.)

F. de B. Capello.—Descripção de tres especies novas de Crustaceos da Africa occidental; &c.   Lisboa.   1867.   4to.

Herklots, J. A.—Additamenta ad Faunam Carcinologicam Africae occidentalis, &c.   Leyden.   4to.   (1851.)

MM. Barker-Webb & S. Berthelot. Histoire naturelle des Iles
Canaries ; Zoologie, vol. ii.
Crustacés by *M. Brullé.* Paris. 4to. (1835–44.)

Besides the special memoirs included in the above list, certain
species are incidentally referred to in works and memoirs not
specially devoted to the West African fauna, some of these are
mentioned by Dr. Studer in the introduction to his memoir cited
above. A species especially worthy of mention as eaten by the
natives of the Camaroons (where it appears in prodigious numbers
in the rivers) is *Callianassa turnerana*, a macrurous fossorial
Crustacean. White described and excellently figured this species
in the Proceedings of the Zoological Society, 1861, p. 42, pl. vi.

INDEX.

———◆———

79

LONDON:
PRINTED BY WILLIAM CLOWES AND SONS, Limited,
STAMFORD STREET AND CHARING CROSS.

www.ingramcontent.com/pod-product-compliance
Lightning Source LLC
Chambersburg PA
CBHW020252290326
41930CB00039B/1043